EXPLORING NATURE
ACTIVITY BOOK FOR KIDS

EXPLORING NATURE

ACTIVITY BOOK FOR KIDS

50 CREATIVE PROJECTS TO SPARK CURIOSITY IN THE OUTDOORS

KIM ANDREWS

Illustrated by Katy Dockrill

ROCKRIDGE
PRESS

Cover and Interior Designer: Kristine Brogno
Art Producer: Sue Bischofberger
Editors: Katharine Moore and Erin Nelson
Production Editor: Erum Khan
Illustrations © 2019 Katy Dockrill

ISBN: Print 978-1-64152-392-9
eBook 978-1-64152-379-0

I DEDICATE THIS BOOK TO MY CHILDREN,
Caleb, Savannah, AND *Connor.*
MAY YOU ALWAYS KEEP YOUR SENSE OF WONDER,
EXPLORE OFTEN, AND STAY FOREVER WILD.

CONTENTS

THE NATURALIST'S TOOLKIT 1

THE SKY ABOVE:
SEASONS, WEATHER, NIGHT AND DAY 23

THE EARTH BELOW:
WATER, SOIL, AND STONE 45

WILD CREATURES:
BIRDS, BUGS, MAMMALS, AND MORE 67

THINGS THAT GROW:
TREES, PLANTS, AND FLOWERS 89

Letter to PARENTS AND TEACHERS

WHILE EXPLORING IN THE WOODS with my nature class, I watched as several kids worked to roll a rotting log away from a ditch. The kids began to chop the log with the edges of rocks they found nearby. Their work revealed a fascinating rainbow of fungus growing underneath the bark. The children brought me chunks of red, orange, and yellow wood, and we talked briefly about tree fungus before they moved on to their next idea. The kids wedged sticks underneath the log, using them as leverage to roll it. Eventually, they sat on the ground and used the strength of their legs to roll the log down the ditch. They squealed with joy—this is what childhood is all about! As I observe my nature classes and study environmental education, I am constantly reminded of the benefits of being in nature and the innovation that happens when kids engage with the natural world.

This book will encourage kids to draw, create nature crafts, and try science experiments. They will learn to observe, use their senses, grow their own food, identify plants and animals, and so much more. The activities here will complement what your child is learning in school or at home. Older children should be able to work through most parts of the book on their own, while younger kids will need some guidance. Pair each chapter with additional books to extend learning. Some of the activities suggest a nature journal or paper to record what they are observing. The companion book, the *Exploring Nature Journal for Kids*, is a great option.

Each activity will begin with a bit of information, followed by a skills list, materials list, and instructions. You can work through the book in any order, but do keep in mind that some activities are better for certain seasons. I recommend you look through all activities for a general idea then choose the best way for your family or class to work through the book.

Lastly, I want to thank you for seeing the value in children playing, learning, and exploring outside. I hope this book brings inspiration and adventure to each and every child reading it.

Letter to KIDS

MY CHILDHOOD ADVENTURES IN NATURE are some of my favorite memories. I remember climbing the fallen tree in my woods, building forts with my sisters, and lying on hay bales and discovering cloud shapes with my best friend. Nature can be your playground, too, giving you lots of fun ways to learn about the world around you. With time, you will begin to notice the birds singing above you, bright colored moss under your feet, and the mysterious night sky. With the help of this book, you will experience nature more fully and make lasting memories along the way. You will learn drawing techniques, make a toad home, create homemade clouds from soap, try science experiments, track animal footprints, make nature crafts, and more! You can work toward mastering new skills and track your progress by following the Skills Checklist at the back of the book (page 110). These are the skills you can look out for in each activity:

SKILLS KEY: NATURALIST

N oticing (look, listen, smell, feel)

A rts and Crafts (draw, paint, create)

T racking (recognize and follow animal signs)

U sing Caution (safety skills)

R easoning (wonder, think, predict)

A dventuring (explore nature)

L anguage Arts (journal, write, and read about nature)

I dentification (research and identify nature)

S urvival (grow plants, catch food, and find your way)

T inkering (collect, build, make)

Learning in nature is a lot of fun, but make sure to follow the safety guidelines mentioned on page x and always take along an adult or get their permission before going out on your own. Your friends and family are going to love seeing your nature collection and hearing about your exciting adventures!

SAFETY FIRST

Spending time in nature is great fun, but always keep an eye out for the following hazards:

POISON OAK AND POISON IVY:
Avoid these plants or you may get an itchy rash. You can recognize these plants by their clusters of three leaves: Remember the old saying, "Leaves of three, let it be."

LEAVES OF THREE
Let it be

Poison OAK   Poison IVY

BEEHIVES: Bees are busy making honey. Stay back or you may get stung!

WASP AND HORNET NESTS: Wasps and hornets are protective of their homes, and have a painful sting.

Honey Bee HIVE

SNAKES: Stay away from woodpiles and long grass where venomous snakes could be hiding.

Snakes

Hornet NEST

FIRE ANT MOUNDS: Avoid standing on these anthills. Fire ants bite and then sting!

Fire Ant HILLS

WILD ANIMAL HOMES: Use caution when exploring caves and large holes, because an animal could be living inside.

UNIDENTIFIED BERRIES AND MUSHROOMS: Some berries and mushrooms are edible, but many are poisonous. Always check with an adult!

Unidentified BERRIES

TICKS AND MOSQUITOES: Ticks and mosquitoes can carry diseases. Especially during warm months, wear bug spray and check yourself for ticks after playing outside.

Unidentified MUSHROOMS

Ticks

Fast WATER

DEEP, FAST-MOVING WATER: Always have an adult nearby when exploring bodies of water.

Chapter 1

THE NATURALIST'S TOOLKIT

A person who studies nature is called a "naturalist." Jane Goodall, Charles Darwin, John James Audubon, Rue Mapp, and Rachel Carson are just a few naturalists you may have heard of. Do you want to be a naturalist, too? Perhaps you already are! Let's take a look at some activities that will prepare you to explore, observe, and document what you see in nature.

Activity 1: Nature Detective

Activity 2: Look Around You

Activity 3: Use Your Words

Activity 4: Picture This

Activity 5: Map It Out

Activity 6: Take a Walk

Activity 7: Nature Exchange

Activity 8: Cabinet of Curiosities

Activity 9: Out on a Limb

Activity 10: Monet the Naturalist

NATURE DETECTIVE

Have you ever seen animal tracks in the woods and wondered what creature made them? Or maybe you'd like to know more about what lives in pond water, or which plants grow in your backyard. A detective gathers information that helps answer questions just like these. Every great naturalist is a nature detective, and every nature detective needs to be prepared with the right tools! When Jane Goodall traveled to Tanzania in Africa to study chimpanzees, she made sure to pack her bag with a notebook, pencils, a camera, and her binoculars. The items you choose to pack in your bag will depend on what you are studying and how long you will be exploring outside. Here's a look at some of the items that could be helpful to take along.

Skills
ADVENTURING

SURVIVAL

Materials
BACKPACK OR BAG

❶ Choose your bag. A backpack will work best if you are planning to go on a long adventure, and a simple cross-body bag is a good choice if you won't be traveling far and only need to carry your journal and writing tools.

❷ Fill your bag. Here is a list of items you may find useful:

- Nature journal
- Writing and drawing tools
- Watercolor paints
- Magnifying glass
- Binoculars
- Small net
- Field guides
- Whistle (for if you get lost or need help)

- Compass
- Camera
- Twine (for making forts, shelters, and nature crafts)
- Soft tape measure
- Small bags or containers (for collecting specimens)
- Permanent marker (to label bags or containers)
- Pair of gardening gloves (for holding an insect or something icky)
- Small shovel (for finding underground treasures)
- Rain poncho
- Sunscreen
- Bug spray
- First aid kit
- Snacks
- Water

3 Now head outside to see what wonderful nature you can explore.

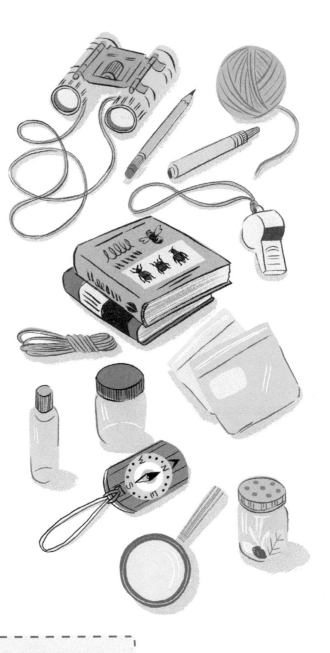

TRY THIS AT HOME
Decorate your bag with patches or pins related to one of your favorite topics in this book.

LOOK AROUND YOU

One of the most important skills you can learn as a naturalist is to be still and quiet, so you don't scare away wildlife. While observing nature you should use your senses, but also use good sense! This means don't touch unfamiliar plants and insects and never taste something unless you have safely identified it with an adult. You should, however, pay close attention to colors, shapes, sounds, and smells. These important details can help you identify what you find. When you observe an animal or bug closely, you can learn where it lives, what it eats, and its common behaviors. Let's see what you notice when you observe wildlife from ground level.

Skills
NOTICING

ADVENTURING

IDENTIFICATION

Materials
CAMOUFLAGE CLOTHING (OPTIONAL)

BLANKET (TO LIE ON) (OPTIONAL)

MAGNIFYING GLASS (OPTIONAL)

BINOCULARS (OPTIONAL)

❶ Find a spot on the ground, sit or lie down, and get a bug's eye view. Imagine using your magical magnifying glass to shrink down to the size of a small bug, and examine the world around you.

❷ Stay still and quiet while you watch for wildlife. Are there grasshoppers jumping by, ants carrying food home, or bees pollinating nearby flowers? Pay close attention to what you see and hear. You will need to remember these details for your next activity!

❸ Now that you know what to look for when observing nature, try this activity in different environments. What do you see by a pond, in the woods, in a tall grassy field, or on a cement walkway? How is the wildlife the same? How is it different?

DID YOU KNOW?

In order to hide from predators (animals that hunt and eat other animals) many creatures will **camouflage** (disguise) themselves. A walking stick bug gets its name from its ability to blend in with sticks and branches. When we camouflage ourselves, we can often observe nature more closely without being noticed. Try wearing brown and blending in with a tree trunk, patch of dirt, or pile of brown leaves!

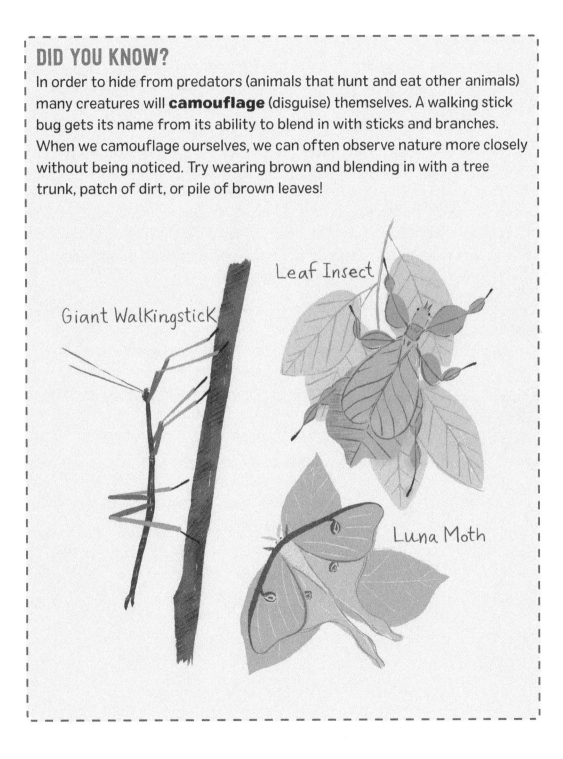

Giant Walkingstick

Leaf Insect

Luna Moth

USE YOUR WORDS

In order to truly study plant and animal life, you need to document what you observe. For example, to find out when nocturnal animals become active, not only do you have to observe their habits, but you also need to write down those observations. This way, you can look back at your notes to reveal an animal's patterns and behaviors. Notes also help you identify wildlife. Let's say you find a caterpillar. Is it green or brown? Does it have spikes? Is it furry? Writing down these important details helps you remember and identify what you saw. It's also helpful to record the date, current weather, and location. In this activity we are going to write about what you saw in Activity 2 (Look Around You, page 4).

Skills

REASONING

LANGUAGE ARTS

Materials

NATURE JOURNAL OR PAPER

PENCIL

1 In your journal or on your piece of paper, make a list of the wildlife and plants you saw in Activity 2 (page 4). These are your nouns. Remember, a noun is a person, place, or thing. Your nouns will be the bugs, insects, and plants you saw while observing from the ground.

2 Now, use adjectives (describing words) to talk about what the nouns were like. Was what you saw black? Thin? Prickly? Shaped like a circle? Did it move slowly or quickly? See the adjective list for more ideas. Write the describing words next to your nouns. Color, shape, and size are important details.

3 Once you've described everything you saw, can you create your own story using those bugs and animals as characters? Will Billy the Beetle eat Sally the Snail, or are they headed to the grassy grove playground to climb and play? Get creative! Share your story with a friend or write it in your journal.

TRY THIS AT HOME

Find an item in nature and, using as many descriptive words as possible, describe it to a friend, parent, teacher, or sibling. Shhh! Don't tell them what the item is before they have a chance to guess!

ADJECTIVE LIST

An adjective describes a noun and might tell us:

HOW MANY: five, few, several, many

HOW IT FEELS: rough, fluffy, silky, smooth

HOW IT SOUNDS: loud, calm, quiet

HOW IT LOOKS: shiny, spotty, dirty, yellow, bright, tiny

HOW IT ACTS: determined, frightened, busy, tired

Example: Seven slimy snails snuck silently through the forest. They were small but brave!

PICTURE THIS

One of the best ways to study nature is to draw it! Drawing what we see is a great way to study the details of nature and keep track of the neat things you find. Naturalists usually write other helpful information next to their drawings, such as the date, time, weather, and location. In this activity, we'll learn four techniques for drawing a leaf.

Sugar MAPLE

BlueASH

POPLAR

Skills

ARTS AND CRAFTS

IDENTIFICATION

Materials

LEAF (OAK AND MAPLE ARE GOOD CHOICES FOR THIS ACTIVITY)

NATURE JOURNAL OR PAPER

PENCIL

CRAYONS

BLACK FELT-TIP MARKER, WATERCOLORS, COLORED PENCILS

(OPTIONAL)

OAK

❶ Go on a nature walk and choose at least one leaf to bring home.

❷ Identify the type of leaf you chose. Write down anything interesting in your journal.

❸ First, try a blind contour drawing. Without looking down at your paper or lifting your pencil, look at your leaf and begin to draw its outline and then the center details of its veins and stem. This is a good technique to use if you need to sketch something really quickly before it moves away, like a bird or squirrel.

❹ Next, place the leaf on your paper, hold it still, and trace its border, creating an outline of its shape. After you have the exact shape, you can then add in details and color.

❺ To create a rubbing, place your leaf under a piece of paper, vein-side up. Using a peeled crayon on its side, rub back and forth to bring out the outline and vein pattern of the leaf. Be sure to hold the paper still for better results.

6 Finally, try a still life drawing: This means the object you are drawing is not moving. Look up and down from the object to your paper, and pay close attention to colors, shadows, and lines. Take your time and sketch your leaf carefully. You may want to add color with watercolor paints.

Blind

Rubbing

Trace

Still Life

DID YOU KNOW?

A few years ago I came across a leaf I had never seen before. After some research I discovered it came from a chestnut oak tree. It looked nothing like the oak tree leaves I was familiar with. Soon, I learned there are about 600 different types of oak trees worldwide and over 60 oak species in the United States. Can you find any oak trees in your neighborhood? Look for acorns on the ground and then look up!

MAP IT OUT

When exploring nature, it is important to know where you are so you don't get lost. Our ancestors followed the sun and stars for direction, but today we mostly use GPS or a map. Get familiar with your neighborhood so that you can explore safely. Drawing your own map is a great way to learn your way around. When walking to an unfamiliar place, try drawing or writing down landmarks along the way to help you find your way back. You may also want to map out the way to a special nature spot so you can revisit it easily. For this activity, we will practice mapping what you can see and hear.

Skills

NOTICING

ARTS AND CRAFTS

USING CAUTION

LANGUAGE ARTS

SURVIVAL

Materials

NATURE JOURNAL
OR PAPER

COLORED PENCILS

PENCIL

1 Gather your journaling supplies and find a comfortable spot outside. This could be in your backyard, at a neighbor's house, in a local park, downtown, or at your favorite spot in the woods.

2 First, map out the physical area. Choose one colored pencil to use for all of your physical landmarks. Are there any unique trees? These could be helpful landmarks! Be sure to add in houses, roads, bodies of water, and nearby buildings. Draw pictures to represent what you can see and write in any important details, such as the name on a building or words on a sign.

3 Listen to the sounds around you. The trickle of a creek to your left or car noises ahead can be helpful in giving you a sense of direction. Practice your listening skills by writing the sounds you hear on your map, using words like "people talking," "dog barking," "trickling water," "car horn," or "birds singing."

BUS DEPOT

Cars Driving

People Talking

Bus Rumbling

SIDEWALK

FENCE

Dog Barking

FLOWERS

TREES

Bird Song

HOUSE

Squirrel Foraging

FLOWERS

WILLOW

DID YOU KNOW?

Some of the first maps were created on driftwood, bone, animal skins, and pebbles. Early maps were often local, showing people where things were within a limited area. It was helpful to map out important rivers and common trading routes to share with other members of the community.

TAKE A WALK

A walking stick is a helpful tool when hiking and exploring. You can use your walking stick for balance as you jump over a small ditch or navigate over rocky land. Your stick will also help you clear your path of small branches, vines, or even spiderwebs. Test thick layers of leaves for animals and check the depth of streams or large puddles with your stick before walking through. Can you think of any other ways you could use your walking stick? Here, we'll help you create your own.

Skills

ARTS AND CRAFTS

ADVENTURING

TINKERING

Materials

STICK

SANDPAPER

GLUE

YARN OR TWINE

RULER

THIN-TIP MARKER

WATER-RESISTANT WOOD SEALANT

DECORATIVE ITEMS (LIKE PAINT, BEADS, FEATHERS, AND MORE)

1 Find a stick that feels just right for you. Your stick should be no taller than your shoulders, and about 1½ inches thick. It should be light, but strong and sturdy. A branch with smooth bark is best. Test out tree limbs from the ground on your next walk until you find one you love.

2 Gently sand your branch with sandpaper. Ask for an adult's help if you haven't used sandpaper before. Sanding the stick will prevent splinters and make the stick more comfortable in your hand.

3 Add a handgrip to your stick using glue and yarn or twine of your choice. Figure out where your hand naturally holds the stick. Spread glue over this area and wrap your yarn tightly around it, as many times as needed to fit your hand size. This will give you something to grip and make your hand less likely to slip on the stick.

4 Next, lay your stick down and line up the bottom of the ruler with the bottom of the stick. Mark the inch measurements onto your walking stick using a thin-tip marker, up to 24 inches. This is a great way to measure and observe the ever-changing water levels in creeks, streams, ponds, and rivers.

5 With an adult's help, seal your stick with a water-resistant wood sealant. This will make it last longer and prevent the measurements from washing away.

6 Decorate your stick with paint, beads, twine, feathers, or other items that inspire you!

TRY THIS AT HOME
Tie a piece of string or fishing line to the bottom of your walking stick. Add a fishhook and use your walking stick as a fishing pole for the day!

NATURE EXCHANGE

Flora and **fauna** (plants and animals) vary in each state depending on the climate, soil conditions, and overall environment. The beach, desert, and mountains all have very different plants and wildlife. One of the ways to explore these differences is to participate in a nature exchange.

Skills

IDENTIFICATION

TINKERING

Materials

NATURE ITEMS (LIKE PINE CONES, ACORNS, FEATHERS)

TAGS OR LABELS

BOX, CONTAINER, OR EGG CARTON

SHIPPING SUPPLIES

1 Find a person living in another part of the country who wants to exchange nature packages with you. This could be a friend or family member, or with the help of an adult you can reach out to other young naturalists online.

2 Go for a nature walk and collect pine cones, acorns, **preserved** insects, feathers of local birds, leaves, small animal bones, empty nests, rocks, or anything else you think your nature exchange buddy would enjoy seeing and learning about.

3 Identify and label your items.

4 Fill your container with your nature items. You can use a box, egg carton, or other container.

5 Add in anything else you want to send. Consider a nice letter or card, facts about your state, a nature craft, or field guides about nature in your area.

6 On the agreed-upon date, both you and your nature exchange buddy should pack up and ship your nature treasures to one another.

7 Enjoy receiving and exploring your new nature items! Now that you are familiar with how to set up a nature exchange, you can explore the flora and fauna of all 50 states from the comfort of your own home.

Hazelnuts

Needles

Sand Dollar

Feather

Shell

Echinacea

Seed Pods

DID YOU KNOW?

Mites, spiders, or egg sacs could be hiding among your nature treasures. Placing them in the freezer for a few days before shipping will ensure that you don't send any unwanted guests!

REGULATION CHECK

Before you start, you'll need a little research help. States have strict rules about transporting flora and fauna. Invasive species are a real threat and transporting seeds or other local wildlife can have devastating impacts without proper care. Make sure an adult checks the local regulations about transporting wildlife before you make your nature exchange.

CABINET OF CURIOSITIES

Ancient explorers from around the world collected foods, spices, plants, and animals to bring home. Often kept in cases, the collection, or "cabinet of curiosities," helped people learn more about the natural world and all of its wonders. Build your own cabinet of curiosities to display your favorite nature items!

Skills

NOTICING

ARTS AND CRAFTS

IDENTIFICATION

TINKERING

Materials

SHELF, CABINET, DRAWER, OR BOX

NATURE ITEMS (FEATHERS, ACORNS, BONES, NESTS, SEEDS, ETC.)

MOD PODGE OR ELMER'S® SCHOOL GLUE (OPTIONAL)

LABELS (OPTIONAL)

SMALL GLASS JARS (OPTIONAL)

PENCIL AND PAPER (OPTIONAL)

1 Decide where to store your nature collection. Do you want a shelf of items that everyone can see, or a private collection that can be kept safe and hidden?

2 If you have chosen a box or drawer to hold your nature collection, decorate it with dried leaves, flowers, and plants. You can glue these items on gently using Mod Podge or watered down Elmer's glue. (Don't glue decorations on a piece of furniture, like a cabinet or shelf, unless an adult says it's okay.)

3 Fill your special container with your nature treasures. Small glass jars are perfect for storing insects, butterfly wings, and fragile specimens. Identify the items first so you can teach other curious naturalists about what you have found.

4 Now that you have a space for your nature collection, you can study your items closely, practice drawing them, and share the stories behind each item with friends and family. Maybe they will want to start their own nature collections, too!

TRY THIS AT HOME

If you want to display your nature collection in a more unusual way, create a nature mobile using a fallen branch, string, and nature items.

OUT ON A LIMB

Tree climbing is a great way to explore the world from a different angle. The feel of the wind, the roughness of the bark, the fresh smell, and the beautiful view from above will stimulate your senses and help you discover things you may not have otherwise noticed. Climbing a tree is very safe when the right precautions are taken. Here we will take a look at some of the steps you can take to be safe while studying nature from the trees.

≋ SAFETY NOTE ≋ Climb only with an adult's permission and supervision.

Skills
NOTICING

USING CAUTION

ADVENTURING

LANGUAGE ARTS

Materials
GOOD CLIMBING TREE

NATURE JOURNAL
OR PAPER

PENCIL

1 Before you climb, learn to climb safely using the CLIMB acronym. An acronym is a word made from the first letters of other words; acronyms can be useful ways to remember important ideas. Study the CLIMB acronym that follows to ensure you are making safe climbing choices.

- **CONTACT:** When climbing, keep three points of contact with the tree at all times.

- **LOOK:** Look for a thick, sturdy climbing tree away from power lines and animal homes.

- **INSPECT:** Fungus and missing bark could mean a weak, decaying, or dead tree. Do not climb.

- **MOVE:** Move slowly and carefully, staying near the trunk of the tree.

- **BRANCHES:** Make sure branches are strong, thick, and alive. Dead, brittle branches can break easily—these may be missing bark.

2 When you have found a safe tree, begin your climb. Stay close to the tree trunk, and keep three points of contact with the tree at all times (for example, two hands and one foot). Before

putting your weight on a branch, make sure it is thicker than the width of your leg and appears strong and sturdy.

3 When you are in a comfortable place, sit quietly and observe nature from above. Here you will have a closer look at birds, squirrels, and bugs that may be crawling by. Don't let them startle you!

4 Climb down from the tree slowly. If your path up the tree felt safe, then try to follow the same path down. Take your time and test your footholds carefully before lowering yourself.

Can you use the word "climb" as an acronym to describe what you saw while observing nature from above? Here's my example:

- Crawling
- Little
- Insects
- Munching
- Bark

5 If you are unable or prefer not to climb a tree, you could observe from underneath a tree looking up, or from a closed second-story window or a balcony.

DID YOU KNOW?

Goats are excellent tree climbers! In Morocco, goats sometimes climb to the tops of argan trees for their delicious fruit. Argan oil is mostly manufactured by hand now, but traditionally, the fruit's seeds were collected from the goat's droppings, making the seeds softer and easier to process.

MONET THE NATURALIST

Famous painter Claude Monet once said, "I perhaps owe having become a painter to flowers." Monet was born in 1840, and spent the last 30 years of his life working on a series of paintings called "Water Lilies." The series includes about 250 oil paintings inspired by the gardens and pond near Monet's French village home. Monet loved the way the sky reflected onto the water, giving it life and movement. He was not only an artist, but a naturalist as well. For this project, you'll need a garden or pond to observe.

Skills

NOTICING

ARTS AND CRAFTS

ADVENTURING

LANGUAGE ARTS

Materials

NATURE JOURNAL
OR PAPER

PENCIL

ART SUPPLIES
(PAINTS, OIL PASTELS,
OR COLORED PENCILS)

1 Learn more about Claude Monet using books from the library or sources online. Write down three interesting things about Monet in your nature journal.

2 Find a pond or garden to explore with an adult. Use your naturalist skills to make observations. What do you see, hear, and smell? What adjectives can you use to describe the pond or garden?

3 Now it's time to re-create one of Monet's paintings. Choose a favorite Monet painting from a book or online. Do your best to draw or paint something similar. Imitating the work of famous painters is a helpful way to practice art skills.

DID YOU KNOW?

Some of the most influential painters, musicians, and writers were inspired by nature. Famous poets such as Ralph Waldo Emerson, Henry David Thoreau, Walt Whitman, and Emily Dickinson all loved nature and wrote about it often.

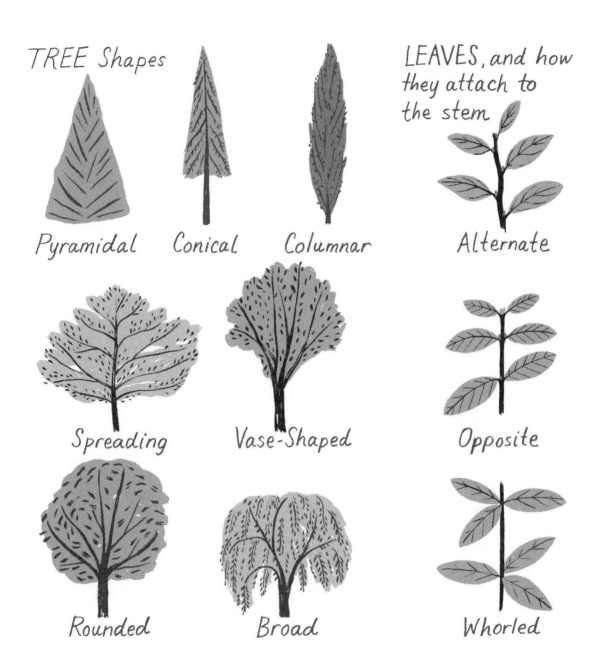

TREE Shapes

Pyramidal   Conical   Columnar

Spreading   Vase-Shaped

Rounded   Broad

LEAVES, and how they attach to the stem

Alternate

Opposite

Whorled

What kinds of trees do you see as you observe your garden or pond?
How do trees play a role in the Monet image you choose to draw?

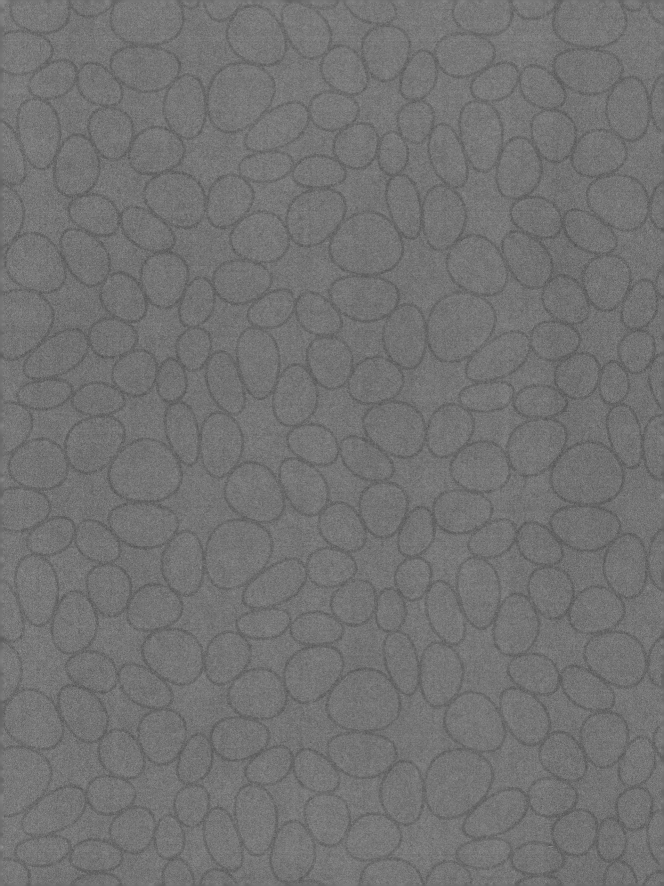

Chapter 2

THE SKY ABOVE:
Seasons, Weather, Night and Day

Learning to read the sky was an important tool for ancient explorers. It helped them predict weather patterns and even find their way in the wilderness by following Polaris, the North Star. In this chapter, you will be learning about some of the fascinating things that go on in the sky above you.

SIGNS OF THE SEASONS

Nature gives us many signs as the seasons begin to change. Each season brings its own special gifts: Bare winter trees for bird-watching, spring flowers, summertime fireflies, and colorful autumn leaves are some favorites. Take time daily to notice the ever-changing world around you. One of the best ways to observe these changes is to befriend a tree!

Skills

NOTICING

LANGUAGE ARTS

IDENTIFICATION

Materials

FAVORITE TREE

NATURE JOURNAL
OR PAPER

PENCIL

1 Find a tree that feels special to you. Your tree can be anywhere, but choose a place you can visit fairly often. A deciduous tree (one that loses its leaves in winter) will have more seasonal changes to observe. Its leaves will change color every fall and regrow in the spring, unlike coniferous (evergreen) trees.

2 Spend some time underneath your tree observing the look and feel of the bark, the color and shape of the leaves, and the insects and birds that may be visiting. Can you identify your tree?

3 Try to visit your tree at least once a month. Do certain birds visit year-round, while others only appear in the spring? Does your tree produce flowers? How about acorns? Notice as your tree shows you the signs of the changing seasons. Write in your journal about the changes you observe.

CHANGING SEASONS

We have seasons because of the Earth's tilt. The Earth rotates around the sun at a 23½-degree angle. This means that in summer in the Northern Hemisphere, the sun's rays hit us more directly, making it warmer; at the same time, it's winter in the Southern Hemisphere, which is getting less direct sunlight. So if you decide to visit Australia in December, pack your bathing suit and sunscreen!

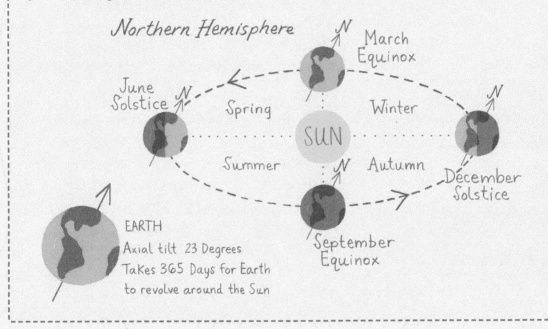

Northern Hemisphere

March Equinox

June Solstice

Spring

Winter

SUN

Summer

Autumn

December Solstice

September Equinox

EARTH
Axial tilt 23 Degrees
Takes 365 Days for Earth
to revolve around the Sun

TRY THIS AT HOME

Decorate your tree for the seasons.

WINTER: Using twine and small sticks, design star ornaments.

SPRING: Create a daisy chain.

SUMMER: Hang homemade bird feeders; see chapter 4, activity 1, for ideas.

FALL: Make a leaf garland by gathering fallen leaves from your tree, poking a small hole in each one, and threading yarn through the holes.

FOR A RAINY DAY

As water vapor rises into the sky (evaporation) it begins to cool down and form into droplets (condensation). As these water droplets begin to combine, they get bigger and heavier and form into clouds. Depending on the atmosphere's temperature, these droplets will then fall as rain, snow, sleet, or hail (precipitation). A sensory rain walk is a good first step in learning to appreciate the water cycle and the rain it brings. You'll need a rainy day for this project.

⇒ SAFETY NOTE ⇐ You should never play in the rain when there is thunder or lightning.

Skills

NOTICING

REASONING

ADVENTURING

LANGUAGE ARTS

Materials

NATURE JOURNAL OR PAPER

PENCIL

1 **SEE:** Often the first thing we notice before rain is a change in the light. Storm clouds may begin to form, hiding the sun and darkening the sky. Observe the sky and watch the rain begin to fall. Large droplets begin to form puddles and streams. Do you see any rainbows or sunrays peeking through the clouds? What interesting things do you see?

2 **HEAR:** Close your eyes and listen to the sound of the rain. Listen in a parked car or under a metal roof. The sound is much louder! Listen outside as the droplets splash, drip, and pitter-patter. What rain sounds do you hear?

3 **SMELL:** Take in the smell of **petrichor** (the earthy scent that occurs when rain first mixes with dry ground). This is usually strongest after a dry spell.

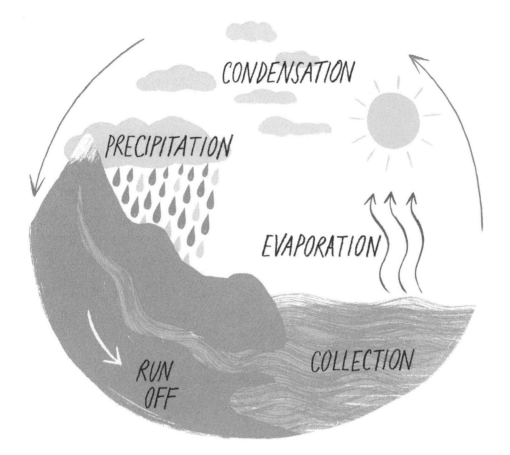

4 **TOUCH:** Feel the rain against your skin. Stand in the rain perfectly still. Now run really fast in the rain. How does it feel different? Do you get more wet or less wet when running in the rain?

5 **TASTE:** Lean your head back, open your mouth, and taste the rain.

6 Write about your sensory experience in your nature journal.

> **DID YOU KNOW?**
> Average-sized raindrops take about 2 minutes to reach the ground and travel around 14 miles per hour.

MOSTLY CLOUDY

Learning to identify common cloud types can help you understand the weather better. Cirrus, cumulus, stratus, and nimbus are the most common types of clouds. The terms cirro-, alto-, and strato- added to the front of these words tell us how high or low the clouds are in the sky. Take a look at our cloud glossary to learn more. You'll need a cloudy day for this project.

Skills

NOTICING

ARTS AND CRAFTS

REASONING

LANGUAGE ARTS

IDENTIFICATION

Materials

BLANKET

NATURE JOURNAL OR PAPER

PENCIL

1 On a cloudy day, head outside with a blanket. Lay your blanket in a spot with plenty of open sky for viewing.

2 Observe the clouds and try to identify their types. What do the clouds tell you about today's weather? Write down the cloud types and your weather predictions.

3 Look for shapes in the sky. Can you find a dragon, an elephant, or a mountain? What pictures did you find? Draw your cloud pictures in your nature journal.

TRY THIS AT HOME

Create your own cloud by microwaving a bar of plain white soap for about 1½ minutes. This will give you a fluffy ball that you can shape into cloud formations. Watch out! Contents from the microwave will be HOT. Ask an adult to help you remove your clouds.

CLOUD GLOSSARY

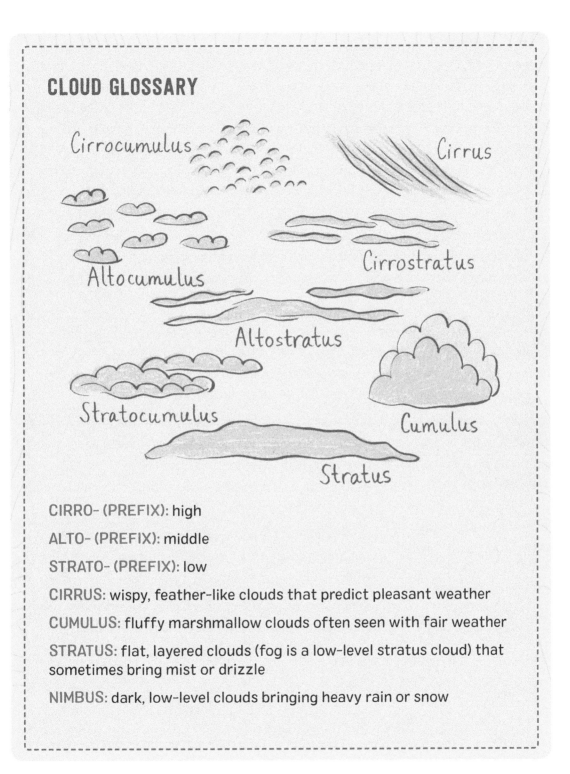

CIRRO- (PREFIX): high

ALTO- (PREFIX): middle

STRATO- (PREFIX): low

CIRRUS: wispy, feather-like clouds that predict pleasant weather

CUMULUS: fluffy marshmallow clouds often seen with fair weather

STRATUS: flat, layered clouds (fog is a low-level stratus cloud) that sometimes bring mist or drizzle

NIMBUS: dark, low-level clouds bringing heavy rain or snow

LET IT SNOW

When ice crystals stick together, they form a snowflake. As the snowflake falls to the ground, its speed and falling pattern work together with the air temperature and humidity to mold it into its own unique shape. The phrase, "No two snowflakes are alike," was first said by Wilson "Snowflake" Bentley, a dedicated snowflake photographer. He would spend hours a day catching snowflakes on black velvet, so that their shapes could be photographed before they melted. Thanks to the work of Mr. Bentley and his 5,000 snowflake photographs, we now know that there are 35 basic snowflake shapes—but no two are exactly alike! You'll need a cold, snowy day for this project.

Skills

LANGUAGE ARTS

IDENTIFICATION

Materials

BLACK PAPER, FELT, OR OTHER FABRIC

SNOWFLAKES (THIS WILL ONLY WORK WITH LARGE SNOWFLAKES, NOT THE POWDERY KIND OF SNOW)

MAGNIFYING GLASS

NATURE JOURNAL OR PAPER

PENCIL

1 The color black gives the best contrast for viewing snow. Place your paper or fabric in the freezer for several hours or overnight.

2 Remove your paper or fabric from the freezer and immediately head outside. Use the paper or fabric to catch snowflakes. This will work best when the outside temperature is quite cold, ideally below 23°F.

3 Examine your snowflakes closely using your magnifying glass. Can you identify any of the basic snowflake shapes?

4 Write about your snow day experience and what you observed in your nature journal.

Common SNOWFLAKES

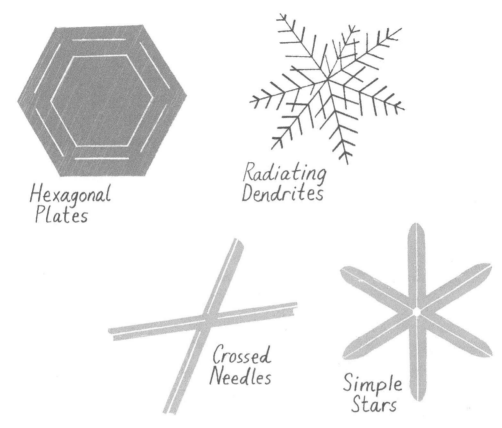

Hexagonal Plates

Radiating Dendrites

Crossed Needles

Simple Stars

TRY THIS AT HOME

☀ Make a snow fairy house using only items from nature. Holly berries, small sticks, pine needles, and pine cones are great for winter fairy house building!

☀ Create a snow insect. Can you use snowballs and sticks to create an ant, caterpillar, or beetle? What else can you come up with?

☀ If you live somewhere without snow, make paper snowflakes or try making play snow by mixing 1 cup of baking soda with 1 cup of shaving cream.

BLOW WIND BLOW

When the sun heats up the air, the air rises, and cooler air moves in to take its place. This causes differences in **air pressure**, which in turn cause wind. Wind is invisible, but its effects aren't. Hurricanes or tornadoes can cause winds of up to 100 to 200 miles per hour. A strong wind can knock down trees and tear through houses. Before modern weather forecasting, wind chimes were a way to determine increasing wind speeds and predict oncoming storms. Let's take a look at one of the many ways to make wind chimes.

Skills

ARTS AND CRAFTS

ADVENTURING

TINKERING

Materials

NATURE ITEMS (SMALL PINE CONES, ACORNS, ROCKS, STICKS, SEASHELLS, ETC.)

STICK (ABOUT 16 INCHES LONG)

RULER

SCISSORS

TWINE OR YARN

HAMMER

NAIL

6 METAL CAN LIDS

HOT GLUE GUN

1 Go for a nature walk and collect items from the ground, like small pine cones, acorns, rocks, sticks, and seashells. You will also need to find a stick about 16 inches long as your hanging stick.

2 Cut 6 pieces of twine or yarn, each about 12 inches long. Cut an extra piece that's 24 inches long, which you'll use to hang your stick.

3 With an adult's help, use a hammer and nail to create a hole in the top of each can lid, removing the nail once the hole is made.

4 Tie one end of each piece of string through the hole in each can lid. Tie the other end of the strings to your hanging stick, about 2 inches apart, to hang the can lids.

5 Tie each end of the 24-inch piece of twine to opposite ends of your stick for hanging.

6 Using your hot glue gun (with an adult's help), attach nature items to the top of each metal lid. You can glue 1 item on each lid or put a mix of nature items on each. Use your imagination and make it your own!

7 Hang your wind chime outside. When the chimes get really loud, you will know that a storm could be on its way!

DID YOU KNOW?

Wind can generate electricity with the help of machines like windmills and turbines. The wind spins the blades of the turbine, which spins a shaft that is connected to a generator, making electricity. The first windmills powered grain mills and water pumps. While some small farms still use traditional wind-mills, wind turbines are mostly used in businesses and homes.

THE WAY OF THE WIND

Long ago, farmers and sailors learned that winds coming from different directions caused a shift in weather. For example, north winds generally bring cooler weather, while south winds bring warmer weather. A weather vane is a tool that helps you find the direction of the wind; it spins and points in the direction the wind is coming from. Build your own **weather vane** to help observe the changing winds.

Skills

NOTICING

REASONING

TINKERING

Materials

SCISSORS

RULER

DRINKING STRAW

2 THICK LEAVES OR A THICK PIECE OF PAPER (LIKE CARD STOCK OR A NOTE CARD)

STICK, AT LEAST 12 INCHES LONG

SEWING PIN

COMPASS (OPTIONAL)

1 Press the end of the straw together and cut a ½-inch slit into the top and bottom ends. (If you drew a line from one slit to the other, it would be a straight line.)

2 Cut a triangle and a square from thick paper or leaves. Your triangle should be about 1¾ inches on each side, and your square should be 2 inches. Insert the triangle into the slits on one end of the straw, pointing outward, and the square in the slits on the other end, to make an arrow.

3 Center your straw horizontally on top of the stick and pin it in place with your pin. The pin should be tight enough to stay in place, but loose enough to allow the straw to spin freely.

4 Head outside and observe the weather. Can you feel the wind blowing? What direction do you think it is coming from?

5 Decide on a place for your weather vane. It will work best in an open space away from buildings and trees.

6 Push your stick into the ground. This will be easiest on a day when the ground is wet and soft.

7 Spend a few minutes watching your weather vane. You can use a compass to determine which direction the wind is blowing. If you don't have a compass, remember: The sun rises in the east, and sets in the west. If your arrow is pointing in the direction where the sun sets, then the wind is coming from the west and blowing east. Check your weather vane throughout the day and see if it changes!

TRY THIS AT HOME

Create a homemade flag to fly in the wind. Cut three or more rectangular strips of fabric, ribbon, crepe paper, or plastic grocery bags. Each strip should be about an arm's length and 3 inches wide. Tie one end of each strip to a stick. Tie the first strip toward the top of the stick and the remaining strips about an inch apart. Fly your flag outside on a windy day.

SKY WATCH

Before modern weather tools were invented, people made weather predictions based on observations. Sailors used the colors of the sky to determine if it was a good day to sail. By watching the sky at sunset and sunrise, some began to believe the old proverb, "Red sky at night, sailors delight. Red sky at morning, sailors take warning." Although this is not very accurate, it does hold some truth. A red sky at night means the setting sun is traveling through a lot of dust particles, suggesting high air pressure, and likely nice weather. A deep, red morning sky suggests a lot of water vapor present in the atmosphere, so afternoon rainfall is possible. In this activity, you'll use these signs to find a good day to sail your own homemade boat.

⇋ SAFETY NOTE ⇌ Always have adult supervision near bodies of water.

Skills

NOTICING

USING CAUTION

ADVENTURING

LANGUAGE ARTS

TINKERING

Materials

BARK

STICK

LEAF

HOT GLUE GUN

NATURE JOURNAL
OR PAPER

PENCIL

1 Gather a piece of bark, a small stick, and a leaf. Try finding a bark piece and stick both about the length of your hand. The leaf should be slightly smaller than the stick. You can experiment with other sizes too, but you want your stick to be thick enough to be sturdy, and not too heavy or your boat will topple over.

2 Fold your leaf in half lengthwise. Poke your stick through the top and bottom parts of the leaf until the leaf is centered on the stick. Now open the leaf slightly to reveal your boat's sail.

3 With an adult's help, hot glue your stick to the smooth, inner side of the piece of bark. You've created a tiny sailboat!

4 Watch the sunset one evening, and the following morning watch the sunrise. Study the relationship between the colors of the morning and evening skies and the weather. Do you predict that it will be a good day for sailing? Record your observations and predictions in your nature journal.

⑤ Take your sailboat outside, and float it in a puddle, pond, stream, or any other body of water.

⑥ How was the weather while you sailed your boat? Did the colors of the sky give an accurate forecast? Record the results in your nature journal.

TRY THIS AT HOME

Dusk, right before nightfall, is an incredible time to watch the sky. When the sun is near the horizon, its light has to travel through more of the atmosphere to reach our eyes. This process softens the sun's light, creating a lovely warm glow in the sky. Photographers call this "the golden hour." As night is approaching, the skies are full of excitement. Look for:

TREETOPS highlighted by the sun

BATS heading out for their nightly dinner

AIRPLANES glowing across the sky

THE MOON rising

STARS appearing

THE SUN setting

COLORFUL SKIES

AROUND THE CLOCK

Early clocks were called shadow clocks or sundials. A stick or pillar, called a **gnomon**, would cast a shadow of different lengths and directions depending on the sun's position in the sky. This information was then used to determine an estimated time. Today, we'll look at a basic sundial design. This activity will work best if you can be at home from sunrise to sunset.

Skills

NOTICING

REASONING

SURVIVAL

TINKERING

Materials

STICK (ABOUT
12 INCHES LONG
AND ABOUT AS
THICK AS A PENCIL)

12 SMALL ROCKS

PERMANENT MARKER

CLOCK

1 Go outside and find a 12-inch-long stick and 12 small rocks.

2 Use a marker to write the numbers 1 through 12 on your rocks.

3 Choose a place outside that receives full sun all day.

4 Push your stick into the ground so it stands securely (the stick will be our gnomon). If you live in the Northern Hemisphere, angle your stick north at about a 45-degree angle; if you live in the Southern Hemisphere, slant it south. This is necessary due to the tilt of the earth. If you need help angling the stick, ask an adult for help.

5 During daylight hours, check your sundial every hour on the hour. Using a clock as your guide, place the rock that corresponds with the time on the shadow line each hour. If you begin at sunrise, you will likely be starting with the number 6 or 7. Over 12 hours, the rocks will create a full or partial circle. While outside, also pay attention to the sun's position in the sky (without looking directly at it).

6 At the end of the day, you should have a fun new way of telling time while you are playing outside! Your sundial will need to be adjusted if you honor daylight saving time, as well as when the days begin to get shorter or longer.

DID YOU KNOW?

Certain flowers can help you tell time. In 1752 a taxonomist (a biologist that groups living things, or **organisms**, into categories) named Carl Linnaeus created the first flower clock. He based his clock on his observations of flowers that opened and closed every day at certain hours, like the marigold, Canadian hawkweed, and white water lily.

SEEING STARS

Our galaxy contains millions of stars. Stars are always in the sky, but we can't see them during the day because of the brightness of the sun, our closest star. When the sun sets for the night, stars fill the magnificent night sky. Many ancient cultures observed the shapes and patterns of the stars and gave them names: We call these "constellations." Out of the 88 constellations that astronomers recognize, 40 of them are named after animals! This activity will help you learn some of the most common constellations and their names.

Skills

ARTS AND CRAFTS

IDENTIFICATION

Materials

THICK LEAVES OR PAPER

CONSTELLATION GUIDE
(OPTIONAL)

SINGLE-HOLE PUNCH

FLASHLIGHT

1 Gather your supplies. I like to use thick leaves, like those from a magnolia or persimmon tree, but paper works well, too.

2 Using a constellation guide or the illustrations included here, decide which shapes you want to create. Will you bring to life the Aries ram or the Leo lion? How about Aquila the eagle?

3 Use your hole punch to create the design of one or more constellations on your leaf or paper.

4 While in a completely dark room, shine a flashlight behind the leaf or paper and watch the design appear on the wall.

5 Which animal constellation is your favorite? Can you find it in the night sky? Remember, some of the constellations may currently be below the horizon and not visible. Download a sky map app to easily find and identify stars, planets, and constellations.

TRY THIS AT HOME

Watch a meteor shower!
For a schedule, check https://StarDate.org/Night Sky/Meteors.

Certain comets come into contact with the Earth's orbit at about the same time each year. As the comets roam our solar system, pieces break off, creating small fragments we call meteoroids. These meteoroids burn up as they travel through Earth's atmosphere, creating meteor showers. Set an alarm to wake up between midnight and 4 a.m. on the night of a predicted meteor shower. Find an open field, away from city lights, and lie back and watch the show!

MOON WALK

The mysterious moon has no light of its own; instead, the moon acts like a mirror for the sun, reflecting its light. During a full moon, the entire face of the moon is illuminated by the sun's rays. Although the moon is always the same size, our brains trick us into thinking it looks larger when it first rises above the horizon. Watching the moon rise is a magical experience. Below is an activity to help you light the way.

Skills

NOTICING

ARTS AND CRAFTS

ADVENTURING

Materials

1 TO 2 SHEETS OF WHITE TISSUE PAPER

1 (16-OUNCE) JAR (A LITTLE SMALLER OR BIGGER WILL ALSO WORK)

MOD PODGE OR WATERED-DOWN ELMER'S® SCHOOL GLUE

LEAVES, FERNS, DRIED FLOWERS, OR OTHER PLANTS, FOR DECORATING

CRAFT WIRE

SMALL BATTERY-OPERATED CANDLE

1 Tear tissue paper by hand into roughly 3-inch pieces. You will need enough to cover your jar twice.

2 Paint your jar using Mod Podge or slightly watered-down Elmer's glue.

3 Stick your tissue paper onto the jar.

4 Add leaves and other plants to decorate your jar. Arrange them to your liking.

5 Add another layer of glue and tissue paper on top of your nature items.

6 Wrap wire around the mouth of the jar three times. To make a handle, loop the wire over the opening and wrap the loose end under the wire on the opposite side of the opening. Now you can carry your jar.

7 Once everything is dry, add a battery-operated candle to the inside of your jar and head out for your full moon walk (with a parent's company or permission!).

8 Head out early enough to watch the moon rise (check online for the time). Notice birds heading home for the night and bats becoming active. Once it is dark, look for spiders spinning a web, beavers at work in the river, lightning bugs, owls, moths, bats hunting for dinner, and more.

PHASES OF THE MOON

When the sunlit portion of the moon is growing, it's called waxing; when that part is getting smaller, it's called waning. After the new moon (when we can't see the moon at all), it returns as a waxing crescent, when less than half of the moon is lit. When more than half is lit up, it's called a waxing gibbous moon. After the full moon (when the whole face of the moon is lit) it begins to wane. The waning gibbous moon is followed by the waning crescent and then the new moon. This lunar cycle is 29½ days long.

Chapter 3

THE EARTH BELOW:
Water, Soil, and Stone

If you were to peel away the layers of the earth like an onion, the outside would be the **Earth's crust** (where we live), followed by the **mantle, outer core**, and **inner core**. Rocks, water, and soil, along with many elements (such as oxygen and iron), make up our planet Earth. Let's take a closer look.

CATCH AND RELEASE

Water covers about 71 percent of Earth's surface, and it's full of living creatures. Before grocery stores, if you wanted to eat fish, you had to catch it yourself in a lake, river, or the sea. Some of the first fish traps were created using vines; they took many hours to make. To make a fish trap today, all you need is a plastic bottle and a few supplies, plus a slow-moving creek, river, pond, or lake.

Skills

ADVENTURING

IDENTIFICATION

SURVIVAL

TINKERING

Materials

SCISSORS

16-OUNCE BOTTLE (FOR CATCHING MINNOWS)

TWINE (AT LEAST 16 INCHES LONG)

MINNOW BAIT (BITS OF HOT DOG, BACON, CAT OR DOG FOOD, BREAD, OR EVEN CHEETOS!)

STAPLER

1 With an adult's help, cut the top portion off of a 16-ounce bottle (just above the label). Remove the bottle cap; also remove the plastic ring below it and the label for the safety of the water animals. Set aside the top piece.

2 Using the tip of the scissors, have an adult help you make a small hole on both sides of the bottom of the bottle. To make a handle, thread a piece of twine or thin rope through the holes. Tie each end of the twine in a knot big enough that it doesn't slip back through the hole.

3 Place bite-size pieces of bait in the bottle.

4 Take the bottle top and flip it upside down. Push it into the bottle until the cut edges line up.

5 Staple around the top edge to secure the two pieces together.

6 Place your trap in a slow-moving creek, river, pond, or lake. It should be completely underwater. I like to wrap the handle around a low branch or rock to keep it from floating away.

7 Wait 3 to 5 hours (or overnight) and come back to check your trap. What did you catch? Your fish trap will likely catch small minnows. Observe the fish closely. Can you find the gills where the minnow's head and body connect? The gills allow the fish to breathe underwater. Once your observation is com-plete, you can release your minnows back into the water.

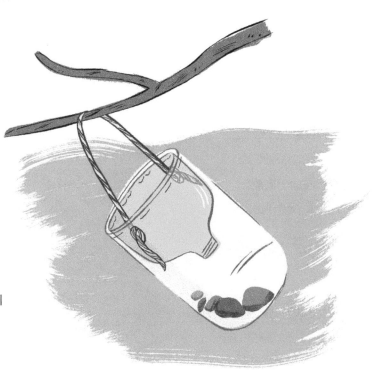

8 Rinse your trap with clean water and store it until next time. Be sure to **recycle** your fish trap when the time comes. We don't want plastic in our waters!

DID YOU KNOW?

Everything on Earth needs water to live, but sadly about 14 billion pounds of trash are dumped into the oceans every year. That is why it is so important that we don't litter (throw trash on the ground or in water). You can help pre-vent water **pollution** by recycling your trash and picking up other people's litter from the ground; this way, it doesn't get washed into the water where it can harm fish and other wildlife.

SINK OR FLOAT?

It is surprising that something as big and heavy as a ship can float, but a small penny will sink. How is this possible? The long, wide base of the ship **displaces** more water than the penny. The more water an object displaces, the greater the pressure pushing it up toward the surface. That upward pressure helps these objects float.

Skills

REASONING

ADVENTURING

LANGUAGE ARTS

Materials

SMALL BASKET OR BAG

NATURE ITEMS (ACORNS, PINE CONES, PEBBLES, LEAVES, SEEDS, ETC.)

MEDIUM BOWL

WATER

NATURE JOURNAL OR PAPER

PENCIL

MEASURING CUPS

TABLE SALT (1 TABLESPOON PER CUP OF WATER)

TABLESPOON

1 Grab your basket and head outside to explore. Collect nature items in your basket. Look for small pieces of bark, seedpods, leaves, acorns, rocks, pine cones, and more.

2 Once home, sort your nature items into two piles: the items that you think will float, and the ones that you think will sink.

3 Fill a medium-size bowl with water.

4 Place each item into the bowl to test your **hypothesis** (educated guess) about whether it will sink or float. Record your results in your nature journal.

5 Dump out the water and refill your bowl with warm water, mixing in table salt until dissolved (1 tablespoon per cup of water).

6 Place your nature items back into the bowl one at a time. How does this change your results? Record the second-round results in your journal.

TRY THIS AT HOME

Do you think an orange will float or sink in water? Fill a tall vase or large bowl with water, and place your orange inside. Next, take out the orange, peel it, and place it back into the water. Are you surprised by your results? Just like a life jacket helps you float, the air pockets in the orange peel help it float!

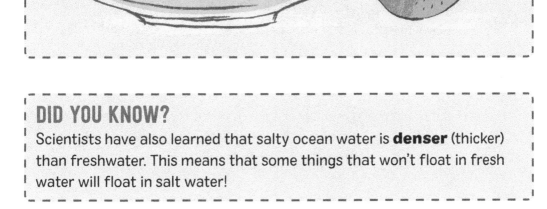

DID YOU KNOW?

Scientists have also learned that salty ocean water is **denser** (thicker) than freshwater. This means that some things that won't float in fresh water will float in salt water!

MAGNIFYING GLASS (OF WATER!)

Have you ever looked through a glass of water and noticed that the items on the other side look magnified (bigger)? The **refraction** of light rays, as well as the curve of water in the glass, will cause items to look larger than they really are. You can get this same effect by placing a drop of water on an old newspaper or words in a magazine. The dome shape of the water drop bends the light, causing the tiny letters to look larger.

Skills

NOTICING

REASONING

Materials

BASKET OR BAG

4 OR MORE NATURE ITEMS

4 GLASS JARS OR CUPS

WATER

PENCIL

1 Collect four or more nature items in your basket. Use what you learned in the activity Sink or Float (page 48) to choose items that will sink. Items that float won't work for this activity.

2 Fill your glass jars with cool water.

3 Add one nature item to each jar.

4 Look into the glass from the side, not the top. Do you notice the magnification?

5 With the permission of an adult, find an item in your home with letters on it that can be placed into the jar of water. Pencils work well! Place the item in just long enough to see the magnifying effect, and then remove it.

6 You can also try holding up items behind the glass of water and observing the changes through the glass.

COLD AS ICE

Water in its solid form is called ice. Whenever the temperature drops below 32°F, water changes from liquid to solid. When this change happens in the atmosphere, it brings sleet or hail; when it happens in the ocean, you see icebergs; on snowy land, there are glaciers; and at home, we have ice in our freezers! Here, we'll create ice sun-catchers and study the transformation of water into ice.

Skills

ARTS AND CRAFTS

REASONING

LANGUAGE ARTS

Materials

NATURE ITEMS
(LEAVES, FLOWERS,
HOLLY BERRIES, PINE
NEEDLES, FERNS, ETC.)

MUFFIN TIN OR SMALL
CONTAINERS

WATER

STRING

NATURE JOURNAL
OR PAPER

PENCIL

1 Go for a nature walk and collect some treasures from the ground, such as leaves, flowers, holly berries, pine needles, and ferns. You can also use items from the kitchen like cranberries or thinly sliced lemons or oranges.

2 Place your nature items into the cups of your muffin tin or your containers. Don't use too many in one cup or container, or the light won't be able to shine through.

3 Fill your cups or containers with water.

4 Add a looped piece of yarn or string to the top of each cup or container, with the ends of the loops in the water and the rest hanging out. These will be used to hang your sun catcher.

5 Place the muffin tin or containers in the freezer; be careful not to spill!

6 How long do you think it will take your water to freeze? Minutes, hours, days? Write down your hypothesis (educated guess) in your nature journal.

7 Once frozen, remove your sun catchers from the muffin tin or containers (running them under warm water will help loosen them up) and hang them on a branch outside. Record the temperature and weather conditions in your nature journal. If the temperature is above freezing, how long do you think it will take for them to melt? Write your hypothesis in your journal.

8 Watch the sun's rays shine through the ice and observe the ice slowly begin to drip and melt. Notice how the ice melts faster on warmer days and slower on colder days. If the temperature is below 32 degrees, your ice won't melt at all! Record the final results in your journal, and see how close your hypotheses were.

TRY THIS AT HOME

Place one end of a small stick in the center of a plastic container; Tupperware dishes work great! Anchor your stick standing straight up by placing a few long pieces of tape across the container. Add water to the container and freeze until solid. Remove your ice block from its container and head outside. Fold a leaf in half lengthwise and push it onto your stick. Open the leaf slightly to create a sail for your ice boat. Float your boat in a puddle, stream, pond, or even the bathtub or sink. Try water at different temperatures. Notice how the ice melts faster in warmer water.

MAKE IT WITH MUD

Dirt is made up of tiny pieces of rock, sand, clay, and other **organic matter**, all mixed together. The type of dirt in your area depends not only on these ingredients, but also on the weather. All dirt has at least one thing in common, however: When you mix it with water, you get mud! This gooey, sticky mud can be a lot of fun.

Skills

ARTS AND CRAFTS

ADVENTURING

Materials

MUD OR DIRT

WATER

MUFFIN TIN, BOWLS, CUPS
(OPTIONAL)

NATURE ITEMS (SMALL STICKS, BERRIES, LEAVES, FLOWERS, ACORNS, PINE CONES, MOSS, AND MORE)
(OPTIONAL)

OLD PAINT BRUSH
(OPTIONAL)

1 Find a muddy area or make your own by adding water to dirt (add a little at a time until you get the type of mud you're looking for).

2 Try one or more of the following ideas:

- **MUD BAKERY:** Make mud pies, cookies, cupcakes, and ice cream (don't be tempted to take a bite, though!). Decorate your baked goods with leaves, flowers, moss, twigs, rocks, and other natural items. Sticks make great play candles for a mud birthday cake!

- **MUD PAINTING:** Collect dirt from various locations for color variety. Add water if needed to get the paint just right. Try out your new paint on a smooth tree trunk, rocks, or paper!

- **MUD MONSTERS:** Stick a glob of mud to a tree and create silly faces using sticks, feathers, berries, rocks, or other nature items.

- **MUD BIRD'S NEST:** Add dried grass and moss to a mud bowl to create a bird's nest.

- **MUD SKATING:** With an adult's supervision, make a large mud pit and spend the day "skating" around barefoot. Slipping, falling, and rolling around in the mud are part of the fun! Be sure to clear away any rocks or other things that could get in your way.

TRY THIS AT HOME

Make your own Mud Clay!

Mixing bowl

Spoon

½ cup hot water

½ cup coffee grounds (if using wet coffee grounds, add some flour)

1 cup to 1⅓ cups flour (start with 1 cup and add more until you get the right texture)

1 cup salt

Add the hot water to the coffee grounds and stir to dissolve. Add the flour and salt; mix to combine, and play!

WASHED AWAY

Soil erosion is the displacement, or movement, of the top layer of dirt or soil. During heavy rain, soil is often broken apart and washed away. This top layer of soil, called topsoil, is full of the best ingredients for growing plants, so it is especially important. The layer underneath, called subsoil, doesn't have as many of those ingredients, so when topsoil washes away, it's harder for plants to grow well. Plant roots, mulch, leaves, and rocks are all helpful in holding topsoil in place and slowing down erosion. Let's take a closer look!

Skills

REASONING

TINKERING

Materials

SCISSORS

3 SMALL PLASTIC PLANT-ERS (ABOUT 10 OUNCES, OR 5 INCHES IN DIAMETER; YOU MAY BE ABLE TO GET THESE FREE FROM A FARM OR GARDENING STORE)

3 PLATES OR CONTAINERS (WHITE OR CLEAR WORK BEST FOR SEEING THE DIRT)

DIRT (FROM OUTSIDE), OR A SMALL BAG OF POTTING SOIL

LEAVES, MULCH, AND SMALL ROCKS

1 PLANT (FROM HOME, STORE, OR YARD), WITH ROOTS ATTACHED

WATER

TRY THIS AT HOME
If there is an area around your home where dirt often washes away after a heavy rain, get an adult's permission and try growing grass there or adding rocks or mulch to slow down the soil erosion.

① With an adult's help, use scissors to cut out a rectangle from the side of all three planters. Cut down about 3 inches from the top edge, then over 1 inch, and back up 3 inches.

② Fill the first container with nothing but soil. Press the soil down tightly. This can be dirt from outside or store-bought; just use the same type of dirt for all three containers.

③ Fill your second container three-quarters full with soil and then top it off with a mix of leaves, mulch, and small rocks. Again, press everything down tightly.

④ Place a plant in the third pot. The plant could be grass or something dug up from your yard (with an adult's permission), or a store-bought plant. It just needs to have roots and be large enough to fill the pot. Add soil to the remaining space, pressing it down tightly.

⑤ Lay one container down (on its side) on each of your three plates or containers. The rectangular cut-out should face upwards. Some dirt and ingredients will likely fall out through the hole: simply push them back in.

⑥ Pour 1 cup of water into each planter. This will represent a heavy rainfall. Observe the color of the water that collects in each plate. Notice how the plain soil has the dirtiest water. The plant roots, leaves, rocks, and mulch helped "trap" the dirt and slow down the soil erosion in the other two containers.

BREAK IT DOWN

Decomposition is the natural process of something breaking apart, rotting, and returning to the ground as dirt. If it weren't for decomposition, the world would be covered in fallen trees, dead animals, and trash. Certain worms, insects, and bacteria help with decomposition. The soil created after decomposition is called **compost**. You can create your own healthy soil by composting fruits, vegetables, leaves, paper, and even hair!

Skills

REASONING

SURVIVAL

TINKERING

Materials

ZIP-TOP SANDWICH BAG

¼ CUP SOIL

"BROWN WASTE" (PIECES OF EGG CARTON, PAPER BAG, NEWSPAPER, DRY LEAVES)

"GREEN WASTE" (LEFTOVER FRUITS AND VEGETABLES, COFFEE GROUNDS, GRASS)

2 TABLESPOONS WATER

1. Place ¼ cup of soil into your sandwich bag.

2. Add an equal mix of green and brown waste materials to your bag until it's three-quarters full. Add 2 tablespoons of water.

3. Zip your bag most of the way closed, leaving only a small opening. Use this space to blow air into the bag and then zip it fully closed.

4. Store your bag on a kitchen counter and shake it daily.

5. In a few weeks, your green and brown waste should have turned to soil, leaving you with a full bag of nutritious dirt to use in your garden or for a houseplant.

DID YOU KNOW?

The soil created from composting is called "humus," not to be confused with the hummus we eat! Humus soil has the perfect blend of air, water, and nutrients, making it ideal for growing plants. Composting is nature's way of recycling!

TYPES OF ROCK

IGNEOUS ROCKS begin to form underground, when heat and pressure melt rock into **magma**. Magma usually reaches the earth's surface as lava from a volcano. As the lava cools at different speeds, it forms different types of igneous rock.

SEDIMENTARY ROCKS are created when **sediments** such as shells, sand, and tiny pebbles gather together in layers. Over time, pressure turns these layers to rock.

METAMORPHIC ROCKS are formed when a rock is exposed to extremely high heat or pressure while in the earth's crust. This causes a chemical change, creating a new type of rock.

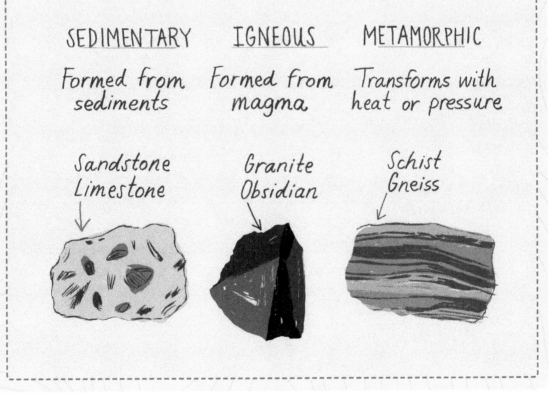

SEDIMENTARY

Formed from sediments

Sandstone
Limestone

IGNEOUS

Formed from magma

Granite
Obsidian

METAMORPHIC

Transforms with heat or pressure

Schist
Gneiss

SET IN STONE

River rocks can be formed from any type of rock (sedimentary, metamorphic, or igneous; for more about this, see Types of Rock on page 59). Typically river rocks start off chunky and rough, but water currents can wear down these rocks over a long period of time, changing the shape of the rock. A rushing river or steady stream will slowly smooth the rough edges, break the rocks into smaller pieces, or even flatten them down. River rocks are great for crafts!

⇒ SAFETY NOTE ⇐ Never go near a fast-moving river, and always have an adult with you.

Skills

ARTS AND CRAFTS

ADVENTURING

Materials

BASKET OR CONTAINER

ROCKS OR PEBBLES (FOUND OUTSIDE OR BOUGHT AT A CRAFT OR LANDSCAPING STORE)

SMALL TWIGS

GLUE (GORILLA GLUE OR A HOT GLUE GUN WORKS WELL; GET AN ADULT'S HELP)

CARD STOCK PAPER OR WOOD SLICE

❶ Take a nature walk and collect any small, smooth stones you find. Do you have a shallow, slow-moving river or creek nearby? Or maybe a ditch or gully that rain water runs through? These are great places to check—though remember, always be careful around running water.

❷ Collect your rocks in a basket or container.

❸ Once you return home, create art using your smooth stones and twigs. You can create a family picture, or perhaps an animal, like a fish, dog, bird, butterfly, or snake.

❹ With the help of an adult, glue your final design to your paper or wood so you can display it or give it to someone as a gift!

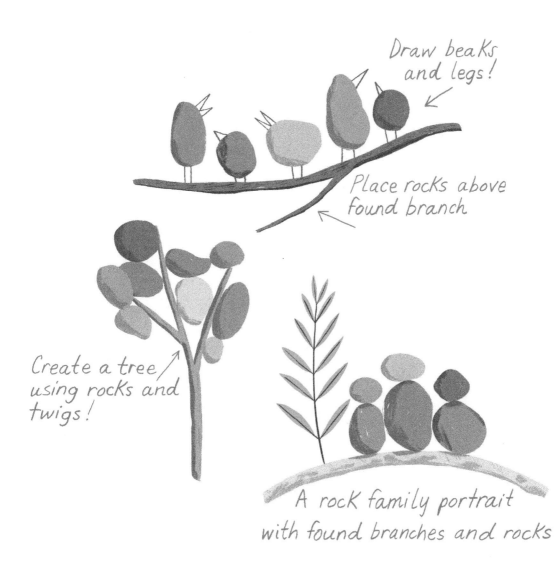

Draw beaks and legs!

Place rocks above found branch

Create a tree using rocks and twigs!

A rock family portrait with found branches and rocks

DID YOU KNOW?

Chalk is a sedimentary rock that's created deep in the ocean. Its main ingredient is calcium carbonate, a type of limestone. In the United Kingdom you can visit a place called The Needles, where three blocks of chalk stand about 100 feet above the water.

HIDDEN TREASURE

Gemstones form from all three main rock types. The heat and pressure beneath the earth can create crystals. Sometimes these crystals are mixed into rocks, but other times they break off on their own. Depending on the cooling time and elements present, these crystals will form together in different patterns, creating beautiful gemstones. Gemstones are usually identified by their color and hardness. They can be used in jewelry or saved in a collection.

Skills

IDENTIFICATION

TINKERING

Materials

1 OR MORE WHOLE WALNUTS

BUTTER KNIFE

SPOON

HOT GLUE GUN

1 WIDE RUBBER BAND

TINY GEMSTONES (PURCHASE IN MUSEUM GIFT SHOPS, ONLINE, OR COLLECT YOUR OWN BY VISITING A GEMSTONE MINE)

MOSS (OPTIONAL)

1 Collect whole walnuts (still in their shell) from a nearby yard, farmer's market, or grocery store. You will need at least one walnut, but it is best to get extras in case they break. Try to find some that are beginning to crack at the top. These will be easier to open.

2 With the help of an adult, place a butter knife in the top opening of the walnut and twist. This should split the walnut along the edges, allowing the two sides to fully separate. It may take a few broken walnuts to get it right!

3 Use a spoon to scoop out the walnut pieces from the shell.

4 Again with an adult's help, add a drop of hot glue to the back of one shell and attach a section of your rubber band. This will prevent your rubber band from slipping when you wrap it around your walnut.

5 Place tiny gemstones inside one shell. These will be kept loose so you can take them out when you want. Can you identify the gems you chose?

6 Glue moss into the inside of the other shell if desired. You may also leave it empty.

7 Place your shell pieces back together, and wrap your rubber band around the walnut treasure box to keep it closed. Open it up anytime you want to inspect your treasures!

TRY THIS AT HOME

Walnut treasure boxes make wonderful gifts. Deliver them to friends and family filled with a special tiny note, candy, gems, or anything else that will fit inside! If you want them to look like regular walnuts, just leave off the rubber band and seal the two halves together with a few drops of Elmer's glue around the inside edge. The treasure box can be easily reopened using the butter-knife trick in step 2.

Raw Ruby

Agate

Quartz

Aventurine

Rose Quartz

Sodalite

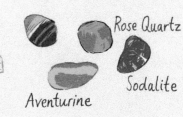

BAKE YOUR OWN FOSSILS

Fossils can help scientists learn information about plants and animals that are extinct. **Paleontologists** are scientists who know a lot about fossils! By studying fossils, they can learn about living creatures from long ago. Paleontologists may be able to figure out the exact shape of an animal they have never seen, what it ate, how it walked, where it lived, or even how it died. Here, you'll create your own "fossils" in the kitchen.

⇒ SAFETY NOTE ⇐ Ask for a parent's permission or help before using the oven.

Skills

ARTS AND CRAFTS

IDENTIFICATION

Materials

BAKING SHEET

ALUMINUM FOIL

2 MIXING BOWLS

MEASURING CUPS

1¼ CUPS ALL-PURPOSE FLOUR, PLUS MORE FOR DIPPING

½ TEASPOON BAKING SODA

¼ TEASPOON BAKING POWDER

⅓ CUP BUTTER, SOFTENED

⅔ CUP GRANULATED SUGAR

1 TABLESPOON POWDERED SUGAR

1 EGG

½ TEASPOON VANILLA EXTRACT

ITEMS FOR CREATING FOSSIL IMPRINTS (SHELLS, PLASTIC BUGS, AND PLASTIC DINOSAURS WORK GREAT!)

1. Preheat the oven to 375°F (with adult supervision).

2. Line your baking sheet with aluminum foil.

3. Mix together flour, baking soda, and baking powder in a bowl. Set aside.

4. In another bowl, mix together the butter and both sugars, making it creamy and smooth. Beat in the egg and vanilla.

5. Slowly add the dry ingredients to the wet ingredients and continue to mix until all the ingredients come together.

6. Using clean hands, roll the dough into tablespoon-size balls and place them on the cookie sheet about 2 inches apart.

7. Use items such as small, clean plastic toys (bugs, dinosaurs, ocean animals) or seashells to make imprints on your cookies. Dip the items in flour first so they won't stick to the dough. These imprints will represent fossils.

8. Bake 8 minutes in your preheated oven. Let cool and then enjoy!

9. Try this activity with clay or Play-Doh for a no-bake option.

TRY THIS AT HOME

Grab your exploring bag and head outside to become a paleontologist. Bring along a small shovel for digging in the dirt and paintbrushes for dusting your items clean. Perhaps you will come across some small animal bones or a fossil imprint on a rock!

Chapter 4

WILD CREATURES:
Birds, Bugs, Mammals, and More

Animals are living all around us. Animals like birds, squirrels, and bees are easy to find, but other creatures prefer to stay a bit more hidden. It can be exciting to spot an animal we have never seen before! If you know when and where to look, you will have a better chance of observing and learning about the wildlife living near you.

FOR THE BIRDS

Birds are not only fun to watch, but they can also help control the insect population. They are **insectivores**, which means they eat insects. Birds also spread seeds, and some (such as the hummingbird) even **pollinate** plants. These are important jobs for helping new plants grow. If you watch a bird closely, you can learn the sounds they make, how they behave, and maybe even watch them build their nest. To really observe birds, attract them to your yard with food and water. Although this activity can be done year-round, winter is my favorite time of year for it!

Skills

LANGUAGE ARTS

IDENTIFICATION

TINKERING

Materials

KNIFE

1 ORANGE

SPOON

4 WOODEN SKEWERS

4 PIECES OF STRING
(34 INCHES LONG EACH)

8 TO 12 STICKS ABOUT
6 INCHES LONG (OPTIONAL)

HOT GLUE GUN (OPTIONAL)

BIRDSEED

NATURE JOURNAL
OR PAPER

PENCIL

1 With adult supervision, cut your orange in half.

2 Use a spoon to scoop out the insides of one half of your orange.

3 Cupping the hollowed-out orange half in your hand, poke a skewer all the way through the side of your orange; then push the other skewer through the side to create an X.

4 Tie the ends of one string to the skewer right where it enters the orange on either side, creating a loop. Repeat with a second string. Use these loops of string to hang up your feeder.

5 If you live in an area with a lot of rain or snow, you may want to add a roof to your feeder. Create a triangular roof with two sides, each made up of 4 to 6 sticks. With adult supervision, use a hot-glue gun to attach one side of the roof at a time to your orange. Use glue to hold the sticks together where they meet at the roof's peak.

6 Fill your orange with birdseed of your choice.

7 Repeat steps 1 to 4 (or 1 to 5, if you want to add a roof) and fill your second orange half with water only.

8 Hang your feeders on a tree branch or by a bush. Watch over the next few days as birds discover your feeders. Can you identify your bird visitors? Keep a record of your backyard birds by drawing them in your nature journal. You can add details such as the bird species, behavior, color, the date you saw the bird, and even the weather.

TRY THIS AT HOME

Birds are more likely to visit your feeder if they feel safe and can quickly take cover nearby. If you don't have nearby trees, try looking for fallen branches on your next walk and bring them home to create a bird shelter. Think of it like building a fort! Once you build your bird fort, you can add leaves to fill the spaces between branches, place plants nearby, or decorate it to your liking. Add your birdseed and water feeders to the fort and watch from a distance as backyard birds enjoy their new shelter.

THE GREAT BACKYARD BIRD COUNT

Bird scientists are called **ornithologists**. An ornithologist studies every aspect of birds, such as the sounds they make, what they look like, how they fly, and their **migration** patterns. Scientists work really hard to track birds, but they could use your help! The Great Backyard Bird Count happens every February all over the world. All you have to do is count birds on one or more days during the bird count. Each day, you submit a checklist of the birds you spotted. Follow the instructions below to participate!

Skills

NOTICING

LANGUAGE ARTS

IDENTIFICATION

Materials

AN ACCOUNT AT THE GREAT BACKYARD BIRD COUNT (CREATE ONE HERE: GBBC.BIRDCOUNT .ORG)

NATURE JOURNAL OR PAPER

PENCIL

LOCAL BIRD FIELD GUIDE OR MOBILE BIRD APP (FOR IDENTIFYING BIRDS)

BINOCULARS (OPTIONAL)

1. Choose a location for observing. Make sure to bring along your journal, pencil, and field guide.

2. Write down the date, weather, and location you have chosen.

3. Sit quietly for 15 minutes in the same spot and write down how many birds you see and what type they are. If you don't know their species, you can use your field guide or an online bird guide.

4. In addition to the bird species, you may want to write down details about the bird's behavior, colors, shape, or even a quick sketch.

5. If you observe in more than one place, you'll need to keep separate records.

6. Log on to your Great Backyard Bird Count account online and enter your bird-watching observations. You are a scientist, too!

FLYING FAR

As temperatures begin to cool in autumn, you may look up and see a flock of geese, ducks, or swallows migrating south. Many birds migrate, or travel, following the warmer weather that brings insects for eating and cozy temperatures for nesting. Other birds, such as cardinals and chickadees, choose not to migrate, and simply fluff up their feathers to stay warm through the winter.

Northern Cardinal

American Goldfinch

Black-Capped Chickadee

Dark-Eyed Junko

Downy Woodpecker

Indigo Bunting

Robin

TRY THIS AT HOME

Create a wooden feather display to show off bird feathers you find outdoors. Have an adult help you drill small holes, about an inch deep, into a branch, scrap wood, or driftwood. Place this in your nature corner and begin to add feathers, pushing them into the drilled holes, as you find them.

INSECT HABITAT

Flying insects such as bees and butterflies are easy to spot as they flutter through gardens, but many insects are harder to find. Look under a fallen log to find bark beetles, termites, and woodlice working together to slowly break down the tree into soil. Pick up a rock and you may find a cricket feeding on fungi. What insects might be hiding in a puddle of water? In this activity, we are going to create an insect **habitat** and take a closer look at some of nature's fascinating creepy crawlies. This activity is best suited for warmer weather when most insects are active.

Skills

ARTS AND CRAFTS

TRACKING

REASONING

IDENTIFICATION

TINKERING

Materials

NATURE ITEMS (ROCKS, MOSS, ETC.)

OLD MUFFIN TIN OR 4 TO 6 SHALLOW TUNA CANS, SCRUBBED CLEAN

WATER

NATURE JOURNAL OR PAPER

PENCIL

MAGNIFYING GLASS

INSECT FIELD GUIDE

(OPTIONAL)

1 Take a nature walk and collect nature items like small rocks, short sticks, moss, leaves, dirt, grass, and seed pods. Look and listen for insects while on your walk.

2 Fill one or two of your tins with water.

3 Arrange your nature items in the remaining tins to create an inviting insect home. Roll a few leaves to make hideouts, make a small teepee of sticks, place moss over small pebbles, or cover dirt with empty seedpods. Who do you think might move in?

4 Place bits of food inside the spaces, like fruit, candy, or breadcrumbs. Think about what the insects will enjoy.

5 Move your insect habitat outside. Try a dark, quiet location, like under a deck or nestled next to a pile of leaves or a mound of dirt. If your insect home will be on a patio or balcony, place it in an undisturbed corner surrounded by other plants or nature items.

6 After a week or two, check your insect home for new visitors. Using a stick or tongs, gently poke around the rocks, dirt, and sticks. Observe any insects you find. Are they eating? Are they working? Are they hiding? Look closely at the insects with a magnifying glass; see if you can identify them with a field guide, if you have one.

7 Sketch the insects you find in your nature journal, and be sure to include their names. Insects have six legs and three body segments called the head, thorax, and abdomen. Can you label these on one of your drawings?

TRY THIS AT HOME

1. Place a piece of food next to an anthill and watch the ants carry it home.

2. Bury an open jar in the ground and leave it overnight. Any insects crawling over the top will fall inside. Be sure to release them in the morning after you journal your findings.

3. When it gets dark outside, place a lantern or flashlight onto a white towel or paper. This will attract moths, allowing you to get a closer look.

BUTTERFLY LIFE CYCLE

Many insects and **amphibians** develop into adults through a process called **metamorphosis**. It is through this process that caterpillars change into butterflies. During the life cycle of a butterfly, the female lays her eggs, and 3 to 5 days later a **larva** (small caterpillar) will emerge. The caterpillar then eats plants for several weeks, attaches itself to a stem or leaf, and then transforms into a **chrysalis** (pupa). In 10 to 14 days, a butterfly will emerge. Metamorphosis means change, and what an amazing change it is!

Skills

ARTS AND CRAFTS

Materials

BASKET OR BAG

2 STICKS, ABOUT 8 INCHES LONG EACH

HANDFUL OF SMALL BRANCHES AND TWIGS

7 OVAL OR ROUND LEAVES

SMALL ROCKS OR SEEDS

WHITE CARDSTOCK PAPER (OPTIONAL)

GLUE (OPTIONAL)

① Take a walk outside and gather materials.

② Decide where you want to build your butterfly life cycle model. You can choose to build it on the ground, on a table, or on a slice of wood, or make it more permanent by gluing it down to a piece of cardstock paper.

③ Cross the two 8-inch sticks, creating a large plus sign. Each area will represent a different stage of the butterfly life cycle.

④ On the top left square, place a few small rocks on a leaf to represent the eggs. On the top right square, use small twigs to represent your caterpillar. In the bottom left square, a leaf hanging from a twig will be your chrysalis. Finally, in the bottom right square, use twigs and leaves to build your butterfly!

⑤ Glue these items to your paper or wood, if you choose.

EGGS

CATERPILLAR

CHRYSALIS

BUTTERFLY

TRY THIS AT HOME

Observing the life cycle of a butterfly is a fascinating experience! This activity is easily done in a jar or netted butterfly habitat, but my favorite way to experience the butterfly life cycle is in a tent! Order an online butterfly habitat kit, or collect your own chrysalises during the warmer months. Your chrysalises can be placed inside a tent (preferably one with netted sides allowing for plenty of airflow). Outside temperatures should be between 65 to 90°F. In 10 to 14 days you should have butterflies. They may even land on you! Provide your butterflies with fresh fruit and a sponge of sugar water. Release them outside after a few days.

FURRY FRIENDS

Scat is another word for animal droppings or poop. People who study wild animal scat are called **scatologists**. Identifying scat can be helpful when you are trying to determine what animals may be living in a certain area. Do you see small pellets from a deer? Or maybe raccoon droppings? Mammals in particular can be a bit shy and difficult to spot, but if you can recognize their poop, you will know who is hiding nearby! Create these replicas to help you learn to ID the most common types of animal scat.

⇒ SAFETY NOTE ⇐ Never handle animal scat, as it could carry diseases.

Skills

NOTICING

TRACKING

USING CAUTION

IDENTIFICATION

TINKERING

Materials

1 RECIPE MUD CLAY (PAGE 55)

❶ Create the Mud Clay recipe found in the Try This at Home section on page 55.

❷ Using the scat ID chart, shape your clay into different types of animal scat. If you'd like, mix in oatmeal or animal hair (perhaps from your dog or cat) to make even more realistic scat of coyotes and other animals.

❸ Once you've gotten familiar with these common types of scat, take a walk in the woods and see if you can find the real thing.

DID YOU KNOW?

Studying scat can tell you what an animal eats. Scientists can then determine whether an animal is an **herbivore** (an animal that eats only plants), **omnivore** (an animal that eats both plants and meat), or **carnivore** (an animal that eats only meat).

SCAT IDENTIFICATION CHART

DEER	RACCOON	DOG
MOUSE	SQUIRREL	RABBIT
OPOSSUM	SKUNK	COYOTE

COMMON ANIMAL TRACKS

DEER	RACCOON	DOG
MOUSE	SQUIRREL	RABBIT
OPOSSUM	SKUNK	COYOTE

F=Front TRACK
H=Hind TRACK

MAKING TRACKS

One of the best ways to discover what wildlife lives in your neighborhood is by learning to identify animal tracks, or footprints. In order to read an animal track, you will need to examine the pattern of steps, the size of the footprints, the number of toes, the overall shape, and the depth of the tracks. A deep print comes from a heavier animal. Do you see claws? Is there webbing between the toes? Are the footprints side-by-side, or diagonal to one another? Using our footprint guide and information from your own research, see if you can identify the animal tracks near your home or neighborhood.

⇒ SAFETY NOTE ⇐ Animal visitors may be a danger to pets and children. Use caution and never feed wild animals regularly.

Skills

NOTICING

TRACKING

USING CAUTION

IDENTIFICATION

SURVIVAL

Materials

FOOD TO ATTRACT ANIMALS (SEEDS, BERRIES, FRUITS, VEGETABLES, FOOD SCRAPS, ETC.)

MUD, WET SAND, OR SNOW

STRIPS OF CARDBOARD (CEREAL BOXES WORK WELL) (OPTIONAL)

SCISSORS (OPTIONAL)

PLASTER OF PARIS (OPTIONAL)

DISPOSABLE SPOON (OPTIONAL)

TRY THIS AT HOME

With adult supervision, visit a pond, lake, or river and look for the prints of birds, beavers, and other wildlife that may have stopped in for a drink!

1 Choose a location for your track trap, like a place in the woods, a pond, or under a tree in your yard.

2 Set out food in your location. If you're close to your house use nuts, birdseed, fruit, lettuce, or corn. This will likely attract birds, mice, squirrels, rabbits, and maybe deer. If your track trap is a safe distance from pets, houses, and play areas, you can pile up scrap food or leftovers as well. This could attract raccoons, possums, skunks, coyotes, or even bears, depending on where you live. Use caution and never feed wild animals on a regular basis.

3 Surround the food with mud, wet sand, or snow. You can dig up dry dirt and add water until it makes a thick, gooey mud. Whatever you use, take a stick or your hand and smooth it out nicely. This will make it easier to see the animal tracks.

4 Let your track trap sit for one or more nights before checking back. Do you recognize any of the animal tracks? Compare them with the chart on page 77.

5 To make a permanent casting of an animal track in mud or sand (not snow), surround the track with a border of cardboard or thick paper sticking up from the ground at least a few inches. This will create a frame for your plaster. Mix your plaster with water until it's the consistency of pancake batter and pour it into the frame until it covers the print completely. It should be dry and ready to pick up in 20 to 30 minutes. You can rinse off the dirt with water after 24 hours.

TOAD HOME

Did you know that toads can eat up to 100 bugs a day? Toads have no teeth, but they do have long, sticky tongues that are used for catching bugs at a lightning-fast speed. During the day, toads like to hide in cool, damp places. They can usually be found under leaves, rotting logs, or large stones. Once the heat of the day passes, the toads wake up and come out for a snack. I don't know about you, but I sure would like a toad or 10 to come eat the pesky mosquitoes, flies, and ants in my yard. Create a toad home to get one to stick around for a while.

Skills

ARTS AND CRAFTS

TRACKING

IDENTIFICATION

TINKERING

Materials

1 (6- TO 12-INCH) PLASTIC OR CERAMIC FLOWER POT

SHOVEL

LEAVES

SHALLOW BOWL OR DISH

PAINTS (OPTIONAL)

1 Choose a shady location for your toad home.

2 Dig a hole large enough to bury your flower pot halfway when it's on its side.

3 Place the pot into the hole. Your pot should have a large enough opening for the frog to make its home inside.

4 Add a layer of leaves inside your pot.

5 Provide drinking water for the toad by placing a shallow bowl or dish of water nearby.

6 Although it's not necessary, you may choose to paint or decorate your toad home.

7 Wait a few weeks and see if a toad moves in. You can also find your own toad by checking under leaves and logs. Toads have bumpy, dry skin, not to be confused with smooth, wet-skinned frogs. When you find a toad friend, pick it up (don't worry, they can't really give you warts!) and place it in its new home.

DID YOU KNOW?

Toads and other amphibians such as frogs, salamanders, and **caecilians** have **permeable** skin. This means their thin skin can absorb water and oxygen. If a frog is hibernating at the bottom of a pond, it can absorb oxygen from underneath the water. Unfortunately, this also means that amphibians are more likely to be damaged by chemicals and pollution. You can help by not littering or using weed spray near animal habitats.

UNDERWATER VIEW

Hiding under pond water are thousands of animals and other living things, most of which we never see. Ponds are home to tadpoles, fish, ducks, crayfish, bacteria, and even microscopic creatures. The most biodiverse ponds have lots of different plants growing in them. The plants in ponds are helpful in providing shelter, oxygen, and food for the pond's animals. Surface ripples and reflections on the water make it difficult to see most of what goes on beneath the water. Making an underwater viewer will help us look past the water's surface. Watch closely, and you may spot slimy algae or even a fish swimming by.

⇒ SAFETY NOTE ⇐ Always have an adult with you when exploring water.

Skills

NOTICING

ADVENTURING

IDENTIFICATION

TINKERING

Materials

SCISSORS

CYLINDRICAL CONTAINER (CHECK THE RECYCLING BIN: A COFFEE CAN, TALL YOGURT CONTAINER, PRINGLES CAN, OR OATMEAL CONTAINER WORKS WELL)

PLASTIC WRAP

RUBBER BAND

1 With the help of an adult, use your scissors to cut off the bottom of your container.

2 Wrap plastic wrap around the cut opening and secure it tightly with a rubber band.

3 Head outside for a water-exploring adventure! Choose a pond, creek, stream, river, or lake where you can safely stand.

4 Place the plastic-wrapped end of your viewer into the water, with the container opening remaining above water.

5 Look through the top of your container and wait patiently! Do you see any minnows, tadpoles, or crayfish?

TRY THIS AT HOME

Fill a glass jar with pond water. You will have the best luck finding pond critters if you collect your water near plants or rocky areas. Include some of the muck from the bottom of the pond. Bring your jar home and allow the contents to settle. This means the heavier dirt pieces will stay at the bottom, making the water on top easier to see through. Observe your jar for several days or even weeks. Do you see any water wildlife? Draw or write your findings in your nature journal.

WILDLIFE SCAVENGER HUNT

Can you find out what wildlife lives near you even if you can't see any? The easiest way is to look for what they leave behind. Did they leave behind footprints, scat, a smell, a layer of skin, bones, feathers? A "left behind" scavenger hunt is a fun way to search for clues about what might be living nearby. It could take months or even years to find every item listed below, but going on a scavenger hunt teaches you to slow down and really notice the nature around you.

Skills

NOTICING

TRACKING

USING CAUTION

ADVENTURING

IDENTIFICATION

Materials

BASKET OR BAG FOR COLLECTING NATURE ITEMS

1 Anytime you go exploring, take the time to notice the amazing things around you. Observe the hole that was created when a large oak tree tumbled down. Notice the fungus growing on a fallen branch. Listen for the sounds of birds flying above. It is in these slow moments that you will likely come across an amazing natural treasure. Bring along a basket or bag for collecting, and see how many items below you can find. Use field guides, books, or online resources to find pictures of nature items you are not familiar with. This will make them easier to spot in the wild.

- Partially nibbled acorn
- "Lace leaf" or "skeleton leaf" made by a Japanese beetle
- Empty egg sac
- Animal bone
- Bird feather
- Animal shell (snail, turtle, clam, etc.)
- Owl pellet
- Shark tooth
- Animal claw
- Empty cocoon
- Butterfly wing
- An abandoned bird's nest

❷ Sort through your nature treasures and determine what animals and insects might be living nearby.

❸ Add chosen items to your nature collection.

TRY THIS AT HOME

Animals leave many other signs for us that can't be collected and taken home. Keep your eye out for the following signs of wildlife.

- Mounds of soil left from moles tunneling through the ground
- Beaver bite marks at the base of a tree
- Animal footprints
- Claw marks on a tree
- Pieces of animal fur stuck to thorns
- Game trails (paths of flattened grass from animals walking through)

SNAIL TRAIL

Have you ever noticed a snail trail? During the warmer months, snails can often be found in damp places. They like to hide under leaves, rotting logs, stones, or even garden planters. Snails usually become active after rain and also at night. Snails leave behind a silvery mucus trail wherever they go. Snails produce this slimy trail to protect their bodies as they slide along. If you want to find a snail, you could always try following a snail trail!

Skills

NOTICING

TRACKING

Materials

CONTAINER OR BOX
FOR YOUR SNAIL
(ADD AIR HOLES)

DIRT

LEAVES

LETTUCE

WATER

BLACK PAPER

1 On a warm, wet day, head outside and look for a snail. If you come across a snail trail, follow it! You can also look for snails in gardens, under leaves, and beneath logs.

2 Once you find a snail, place it in your container.

3 Provide your snail with dirt, leaves, lettuce for eating, and a few drops of water sprinkled on top of the lettuce.

4 Remove your snail from the container and place it on a black sheet of paper. You may want to put lettuce or another vegetable on the other side to encourage the snail to move across the paper.

5 Observe the snail trail your new friend has created.

6 After observing the snail for a few days, be sure to return him to his outdoor home.

TRY THIS AT HOME

Beetles also leave behind trails! Some beetle species create beautiful art and elaborate mazes underneath the bark of trees. Take a walk in the woods and look for trees with loose or missing bark. Can you spot the work of a bark beetle underneath the bark? Trace the path with your finger. Does it lead you to the hole where the beetle made its exit?

Chapter 5

THINGS THAT GROW:

Trees, Plants, and Flowers

Plants are living organisms. This means they grow, breathe, eat, and **reproduce**. Plants use carbon dioxide and sunlight to make their own food through a process called **photosynthesis**. As a result, they release oxygen. This makes plants very important to us, since humans need oxygen to breathe. Learning to grow your own plants can help make the world a healthier place.

HOW TO READ A TREE

The small details of trees are often overlooked, but with practice you can learn to read a tree. Examining it closely can give you clues about its life. You may notice a black streak from lightning, or chew marks from a beaver. You can tell a bear once visited by a large claw mark down the trunk. You can also learn to identify types of trees by studying their bark, leaf shape, and even smell! Some trees are bumpy, while others are smooth. You may notice the smell of cedar sap or the sweet butterscotch scent of the ponderosa pine. Our senses give clues that can help us identify the plants we are studying. At first you will need a field guide to help with identification, but with lots of practice you can learn to recognize tree types and even tell their age!

Skills

NOTICING

ADVENTURING

IDENTIFICATION

Materials

TREE

NATURE JOURNAL OR PAPER

PENCIL

1 For this activity, you need to identify and observe a **coniferous** tree (a tree that produces cones, such as pines, cedars, spruces, firs, and cypresses). Find a young coniferous tree about your height.

2 A fun way to determine a tree's age to count is its **whorls**. Whorls are the areas where branches grow out from the trunk and circle around the tree like the spokes of a bicycle wheel. Count the whorls of your tree from bottom to top; each one represents a year of growth. Be careful not to count the small branches in between, as these are false whorls.

3 Is your tree about the same age as you? Record your observations in your journal.

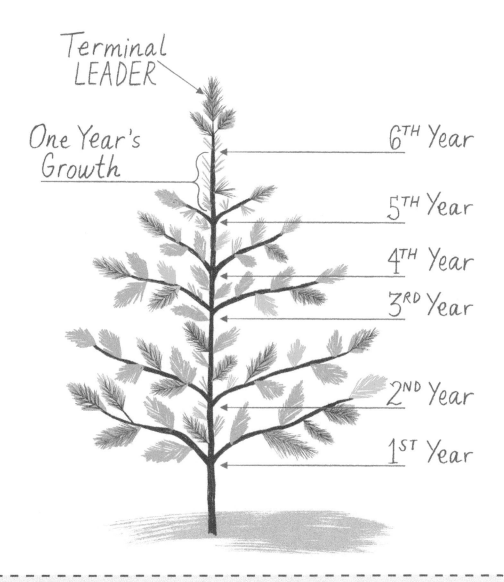

Terminal LEADER

One Year's Growth

6TH Year

5TH Year

4TH Year

3RD Year

2ND Year

1ST Year

TRY THIS AT HOME

Find a small tree branch on the ground (about 12 inches long). Can you identify what type of tree it came from by looking at the bark? Bring your branch home and decorate it. Use items such as paint, markers, yarn, feathers, beads, and charms to make a one-of-a-kind stick. Will you create a sword to vanquish a dragon, a fairy wand, a tool for writing in the dirt, or a baton for conducting an orchestra?

BREATHING TREE

As you now know, a tree is a living thing. Although living things breathe, trees and plants don't breathe the same way we do, by using our lungs. Instead, they breathe through their **stomata**. These are tiny pores, or openings, that allow plant leaves to take in carbon dioxide and let out oxygen. Have you ever seen a tree breathe? Although we can't actually watch a tree breathe, we can do a fun experiment that will allow us to see a leaf's stomata in action.

Skills

NOTICING

REASONING

Materials

LARGE GLASS JAR OR BOWL

WATER

LEAF

ROCK

MAGNIFYING GLASS (OPTIONAL)

1 Fill a large glass jar or bowl with water. The glass will allow you to see the process from all angles.

2 Collect a living leaf directly from a tree.

3 Place your leaf in your jar or bowl.

4 Anchor your leaf to the bottom by placing a small rock on top of it.

5 Place your glass container in a sunny area (preferably outside). The leaf will use energy from the sun to complete the process of photosynthesis.

6 Let your leaf sit for several hours before observing its changes. If you have a magnifying glass, use it to take a closer look. Do you see the tiny oxygen bubbles forming around the edges of your leaf? Your leaf is breathing. Reach in and gently shake your leaf. Watch the oxygen bubbles quickly rise. This is similar to when you go underwater and let out air, creating bubbles!

CHLOROPHYLL makes Leaves GREEN.

DAYS shorten, Less sun, LEAVES change colour.

VEINS in leaves start to close, trapping SUGAR in some leaves, turning them 'RED.

DID YOU KNOW?

During the cooler months, trees prepare for their winter's rest. With less sunshine and warmth, the leaves close their veins and stop creating the **chlorophyll** they need to stay green. Without chlorophyll, leaves will show their natural colors. The beautiful autumn colors of red, orange, yellow, and deep purple have been hiding underneath all year long.

SEASONAL BOOKMARKS

I am always amazed at the plant life that changes with the seasons right outside my door. A surprise dandelion growing toward the end of autumn, new buds reaching out of the winter snow, unfurling ferns growing by the woods—each season brings something new. Many naturalists and artists enjoy collecting nature items like these to use for their creations.

Skills

ARTS AND CRAFTS

TINKERING

Materials

NATURE ITEMS

BASKET OR BAG

CARD STOCK OR BROWN GROCERY BAG

SCISSORS

GLUE STICK

CLEAR PACKING TAPE

SINGLE HOLE PUNCH

CONTACT PAPER OR LAMINATING MACHINE
(OPTIONAL)

TWINE OR YARN

1 Collect nature items around your yard, in the woods, or in a nearby park or field. Flat, thin items will work best. Look for small wildflowers, clovers, ferns, tiny leaves (no stems), and more. Collect them in your basket or bag.

2 Once home, cut your card stock or recycled brown bag into a rectangular shape (about 2½ by 7 inches).

3 Gently glue your nature items onto the paper.

4 Cover the front and back of the paper with packing tape or contact paper. If using tape, make sure it extends wider than the paper. Cut the tape around your paper so you have a ½-inch border of tape around the edge. If using contact paper, cut around your bookmark, leaving a ½-inch border of contact paper.

5 Use a hole punch to make a hole at the top of your bookmark.

6 Add string or twine through the hole and tie to secure.

7 Create a bookmark for each season, and observe what nature items grow year-round, and which ones only grow at certain times of the year.

8 Use your bookmarks in a book, display them, or give them as gifts!

DID YOU KNOW?

Antarctica has only two seasons, winter and summer. The South Pole never gets above freezing temperature, even in summer.

There are some important guidelines to remember when collecting. First, remember the safety rules on page X. Second, only collect flowers and plant pieces from your own yard or places where they are growing wild, such as fields or woods. Lastly, when collecting fresh flowers, ferns, or leaves, don't pull up the roots, so the plant can continue to grow, and take only a few, leaving the rest for others to enjoy.

FLOWER PRESS

Flowers are beautiful art growing outside. Their many colors, shapes, sizes, textures, and smells make flowers a great material for arts and crafts! For many years, people have been pressing flowers between the pages of books in order to preserve them, or keep them looking new and fresh. Today you will learn to make a flower press, allowing you to save colorful leaves, four-leaf clovers, and beautiful flowers.

Skills

ARTS AND CRAFTS

ADVENTURING

TINKERING

Materials

6 PIECES OF PRINTER PAPER

SCISSORS

CARDBOARD BOX

3 THIN RUBBER BANDS AND 2 THICK RUBBER BANDS

FLOWERS AND LEAVES, FOR PRESSING

1 Fold all six pieces of printer paper in half, top to bottom.

2 Use one of the folded pieces of paper as a guide, and cut out three small rectangles of cardboard from your box. Ask for an adult's help if you have trouble.

3 Take the three thin rubber bands and wrap them around the center of one piece of cardboard. Wrap them as many times as necessary for a snug fit. This will be the top piece.

4 Now, make a cardboard and paper sandwich. Place another piece of cardboard on the bottom, followed by three folded pieces of paper, the last piece of cardboard, three more folded pieces of paper. Top this with the rubber band cardboard piece.

5 Add a thick rubber band at the top end and another around the bottom end to hold it all together.

6 Are you ready to explore? Bring along your flower press and collect items as you go. Remember not to pull up any plants from their roots, so they can grow back. You can pick flowers right beneath the bloom or include a few inches of the stem. When collecting flowers, look for ones that are naturally flat, such as violets and daisies. Thicker blooms will not flatten well. The folded inside pages are where you will store your leaves and flowers for drying. Place them inside as you go, or hold them in the rubber bands on the front cover and press them at home.

7 Let your leaves and flowers dry for several weeks before removing. To speed up the drying process, you can store your flower press under something heavy, such as a pile of books. Now they are ready to be used for crafts or home-made cards.

Fold Over

Create a Cardboard Sandwich

Stack Heavy Books

TRY THIS AT HOME

Once you have enough pressed flowers and leaves, you can use them to decorate your nature press. You will need clear packing tape and a glue stick. Remove the front or back cardboard piece of your flower press, and glue down your pressed pieces. Once the glue is dry, cover the cardboard in clear packing tape.

HELP YOUR GARDEN GROW

A wildflower grows without being intentionally planted. Wildflowers are planted with the help of nature (animals, wind, water) and taken care of by the sun and rain. They grow in fields, woods, yards, hillsides, mountains, and on the coast. You can find a variety of wildflowers everywhere! Growing your own flowers makes them a little less wild, but it is great to have your own flowers to cut and display in a vase, give as gifts, or use in crafts. Your wildflowers will also provide food for butterflies, bees, and hummingbirds. For this project, you'll need to visit a garden center.

Skills

ARTS AND CRAFTS

LANGUAGE ARTS

IDENTIFICATION

SURVIVAL

Materials

PACKET OF WILDFLOWER SEEDS

NATURE JOURNAL OR PAPER

PENCIL

COLORED PENCILS OR OTHER ART SUPPLIES

PATCH OF DIRT OUTSIDE OR SEVERALFLOWER-POTS FILLED WITH POTTING SOIL

WATER

1 Visit a garden center with an adult. Bring along your nature journal and write down the names of flowers and plants you like. Talk to a garden specialist about what wildflowers grow well in your area.

2 Purchase a mixed packet of wildflower seeds or individual packets of flower seeds you like.

3 When you get home, draw out a flower garden design in your journal. This can be a picture of the actual flower garden you are planting, or a dream garden that you hope to plant one day. Use your art supplies to make it colorful.

4 Talk to your parent or guardian and together decide on a place to plant your flowers. A patch of dirt in your garden, yard, or the woods works great. You can also plant them in flowerpots or simply sprinkle them around the edge of your yard. You will want to choose a location that doesn't get mowed and that gets plenty of sun.

5 In the spring, sprinkle your seeds in your chosen location. You may want to step on the seeds to push them into the dirt a bit or cover them with a thin layer of soil.

6 Water your seeds regularly and wait for your new garden to bloom. It could take many months to see the flowers grow.

7 Once your flowers bloom, sit back and watch as bees, butterflies, and hummingbirds enjoy the special treat you have grown!

TRY THIS AT HOME

Here are some fun ideas for your collected wildflowers.

- Mix them into pretend soup or use as sprinkles on your mud pies.
- Cut the petals into tiny pieces for a natural glitter or mix up a magical fairy potion.
- Often grocery stores throw away bouquets at the first signs of wilting. Stores are usually happy to donate expired flowers to families for crafts or educational purposes. Ask the manager at your store about this possibility.

INSIDE A FLOWER

Birds, bats, and insects help transfer male pollen grains to the female part of the flower, allowing the flower to create seeds. Without this **pollination**, plants could not produce the seeds necessary to grow.

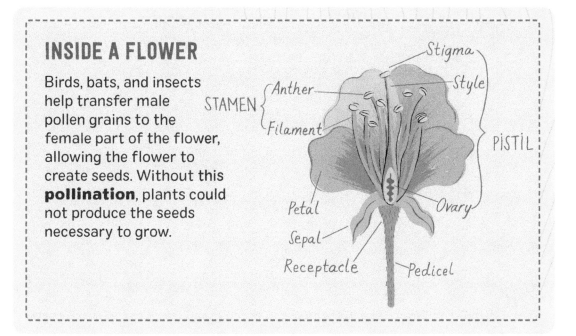

STAMEN { Anther, Filament

Stigma, Style

PISTIL

Petal, Sepal, Receptacle, Pedicel, Ovary

EDIBLE GARDEN

Learning to grow your own food is a wonderful skill. Imagine being able to pick your own tomatoes, basil, oregano, thyme, and parsley for home-made spaghetti sauce; or gathering your own green beans straight from your backyard garden. It is a lot of work to take care of a garden, but also a lot of fun! The fist step is starting your seeds. Some vegetables are best planted straight into the soil after the last frost, while other plants do best starting in containers inside a sunny window.

Skills

SURVIVAL

TINKERING

Materials

HANGING JEWELRY ORGANIZER OR OVER-THE-DOOR SHOE HOLDER WITH CLEAR POCKETS

SMALL HAND SHOVEL

POTTING SOIL

WATER

VEGETABLE AND/OR FLOWER SEEDS (A FEW OF MY FAVORITES: GREEN BEAN, CHIVE, MINT, OREGANO, LEMON BALM, AND MARIGOLD)

PERMANENT MARKER

SPRAY BOTTLE OF WATER

RULER

NATURE JOURNAL OR PAPER

PENCIL

1 Hang the organizer outside on a low branch or fence to make for easier filling.

2 Use your shovel or hands to add soil to each pocket; fill half to three-quarters full.

3 Pour enough water into each pocket to thoroughly dampen the soil.

4 Add your seeds by pushing them into the soil. Read each packet for information on how deep to plant each type. You can plant something different in each row or have a random mix throughout, but I recommend using a permanent marker to label each pocket with the seed type as you go.

5 Bring your plants inside and hang your organizer on a curtain rod in front of the window or in a sunny area.

6 Water your plants regularly by spraying the soil and new sprouts as the soil becomes dry.

7 After 7 days, measure your tallest sprout, draw the plant in your nature journal, and write down its name and measurement. Measure the same plant again on day 15. How many more inches did it grow?

8 When your plants are several inches tall, transplant them to larger containers or an outside garden bed.

TRY THIS AT HOME

Try starting seeds in a recycled container. Here are some ideas:

- egg shells or egg cartons
- hollowed-out orange halves
- old shoes or boots
- empty yogurt containers

A DISHFUL OF DANDELIONS

A weed is a plant that grows where it is not wanted. Weeds usually grow quickly, often taking over other plants and using up the nutrients in the soil. Most of the time, weeds are thought of as a bad thing, but there are actually many good things about weeds, too! Weeds can help stop soil erosion and add beauty to our world, as many weeds are flowers. Some weeds are healthy to eat, and others can be used for healing. Plantain, white clove, burdock, chickweed, and dandelion are a few useful weeds. Dandelions are common and easy to identify. Let's take a look at how this weed can be used.

⇒ SAFETY NOTE ⇐ Only **forage** (pick plants) in areas you are certain have not been treated with pesticides or herbicides and always be sure to wash what you harvest.

Skills

NOTICING

USING CAUTION

IDENTIFICATION

SURVIVAL

Materials

BASKET OR BAG
FOR COLLECTING

DANDELIONS

STORE-BOUGHT
DANDELION TEA

(OPTIONAL)

1 Find some dandelions growing and collect them in your basket or bag. Pick 2 to 5 yellow dandelion tops and 1 or 2 young dandelion plants that are just beginning to bloom. You will only need the leaves from these.

2 Wash your dandelions and leaves in warm water.

3 Now it's time to taste-test your weeds! All parts of a dandelion are edible, even its roots. Try making a salad, mixing in a few dandelion leaves, and topping with petals from the yellow bud on top, or just sprinkle the petals onto your favorite dessert. Yum!

4 If you want to taste dandelions, but don't have any growing nearby, you can purchase dandelion tea from your local grocery store. Add some honey or perhaps sugar and a splash of milk, and enjoy!

DID YOU KNOW?

The yellow bud of a dandelion dries up and soon reveals the seed head underneath. This seed head opens into a round, white, fluffy ball. Pick a dried white flower, make a wish, and blow off the fluffy seed pieces. Every wish made this way scatters hundreds of seeds, many of which will turn into new dandelion plants the next spring!

FUN WITH FUNGUS

All fungi begin as tiny spores and then grow on their food source. This could be mold on an old piece of bread, a bright red-and-white mushroom among a pile of decomposing leaves, or a splash of blue-green color beneath the bark of a rotting log. Fungus comes in many shapes and colors. Can you find fungi growing in your neighborhood or woods?

⇒ **SAFETY NOTE** ⇐ Some mushrooms are poisonous. Do not touch, pick, or eat any mushrooms.

Skills

NOTICING

ARTS AND CRAFTS

USING CAUTION

ADVENTURING

IDENTIFICATION

Materials

THIS BOOK

NATURE JOURNAL OR PAPER

PENCIL

COLORED PENCILS AND/OR OTHER ART MATERIALS

1 Head out on a fungus-hunting adventure. Be sure to pack this book into your nature bag so you can check off your fungus as you find it! It may take months or even years to check them all off, so don't get discouraged. Just remember to explore often and have fun.

2 Here is your fungus scavenger hunt:

- Mushroom with red gills (the ribs under the cap)
- Mushroom with an orange cap
- Mushroom that is taller than 5 inches
- A row of mushrooms growing on a log
- Green fungus growing on a tree base
- Mushroom with spots
- Gooey Jell-O-like fungus
- Crunchy fungus
- Half-circle fungus
- Coral-shaped fungus
- Mushroom containing yellow
- A mushroom with two colors
- An oval-shaped mushroom head
- An umbrella-shaped mushroom head
- A fairy ring of mushrooms (mushrooms that create a circle)
- A rotting log with orange fungus

3 Draw a picture in your nature journal of the coolest fungus you find. Can you identify what type of fungus it is?

TRY THIS AT HOME
Use Play-Doh to create a mushroom fairyland. Add gills underneath the mushroom cap, add a stem, and be sure to use lots of fun colors! Fairies and gnomes will love their new village.

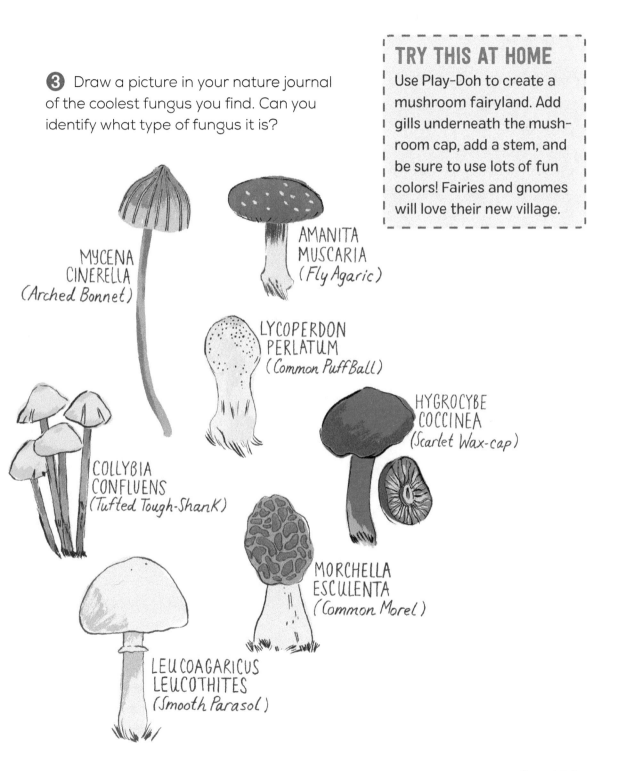

MYCENA CINERELLA
(Arched Bonnet)

AMANITA MUSCARIA
(Fly Agaric)

LYCOPERDON PERLATUM
(Common Puff Ball)

HYGROCYBE COCCINEA
(Scarlet Wax-cap)

COLLYBIA CONFLUENS
(Tufted Tough-Shank)

MORCHELLA ESCULENTA
(Common Morel)

LEUCOAGARICUS LEUCOTHITES
(Smooth Parasol)

SEED STUDY TIC-TAC-TOE

Seeds sometimes travel to new locations with the help of animals, wind, and water. Some seeds stick to animal fur, while others are eaten by animals and grow from their scat. Wind carries fluffy lightweight seeds, and water carries many floating seeds. Some seedpods even burst open on their own, dispersing seeds. Seedpods that fall from trees are a helpful way to identify those trees.

Skills

ADVENTURING

IDENTIFICATION

TINKERING

Materials

BASKET OR BAG FOR COLLECTING NATURE ITEMS

4 STICKS OF SIMILAR SIZE

10 TREE SEEDPODS, 5 OF EACH TYPE

TIC-TAC-TOE PARTNER

1 Today you will be looking for seedpods to use in a game of tic-tac-toe. Bring along a friend, sibling, or parent to play the game with. Head to an area with lots of trees for the most variety. A park with nature trails would be a great seedpod hunting spot.

2 Use your basket or bag to collect four small sticks of about the same size.

3 Search the ground for seedpods that have fallen off of the trees above. Once you find one, you will likely find many of the same type nearby. Examine the seedpod and nearby trees. Can you tell what tree it came from? Can you identify it? Collect as many seedpods as you can, but be sure to find at least two different sets of five that match for a game of tic-tac-toe.

4 Find a spot on the ground or bring your basket back home and play inside. Place your sticks into this shape: #

5 You and your partner will each need five matching seedpod game pieces.

6 Take turns placing your game pieces in one of the squares. The first person to get three in a row wins!

CONE

KEY

ACORN

DRUPE

POD

CAPSULE

NUT

ACHENE

BERRY

TRY THIS AT HOME

My absolute favorite seedpods to explore are cattail and milkweed. Cattails are most often found near ponds, while milkweed can be found in pastures, fields, and on hillsides. If you can't find either of these, consider purchasing them online or finding a friend or family member who can send you a bagful. When you have the seedpods, make sure to open them in an outside area, because these will make a giant fluffball mess! Both seedpods are very satisfying to open, as the fluff unfolds and then blows away with the wind.

GROWING BIRDSEED

In the last activity we mentioned that some plants grow from animal scat. How wonderful it is that something icky, like animal poop, is used to grow beautiful things like flowers, grass, and trees! Birds are one of the many animals that help spread seeds. Some plants contain seeds that are eaten by birds. Birds then fly to a new area and disperse the seeds in their droppings. Did you know that the birdseed you buy at the store can grow, too? By providing birds with seeds, you could be helping new plants grow!

Skills

ARTS AND CRAFTS

SURVIVAL

Materials

SMALL POTTING CONTAINER OR HOLLOWED-OUT ORANGE HALF

POTTING SOIL

BAG OF MIXED BIRDSEED (WITH VARIETY OF SEED TYPES, LIKE CORN, SUNFLOWER SEEDS, AND MORE)

WATER

SCISSORS (OPTIONAL)

MARKERS AND OTHER DECORATING TOOLS (OPTIONAL)

1 Fill the container with potting soil. Sprinkle the top of the soil with birdseed and cover with a thin layer of soil.

2 Water your seeds right away, and continue watering, as needed, when the first few inches of soil are dry.

3 If you have leftover birdseed, sprinkle it outside for the birds to enjoy.

4 Store your plant by a sunny window inside and check its growth daily. You should see small sprouts by the end of the week. Once your sprouts (or plant hair) is long enough, you can cut and style your birdseed hair. Use markers or other craft materials to decorate your pot as you see fit!

5 You may want to move your planter outdoors, and regularly sprinkle new birdseed on the soil's surface. You never know what bird visitors you may get, or where the seeds will travel as a result.

TRY THIS AT HOME

Sunflowers are a wonderful plant to grow for the birds. There are many varieties of sunflowers you can purchase. Mammoth sunflowers will grow bigger than you! In the spring, try planting some of the sunflower seeds from your birdseed pack, or purchase sunflower seed packets of your choice at your local garden center. After your flowers bloom and begin to dry, birds will enjoy the feast of seeds left over. Remaining seeds can be saved for next spring or, with the help of an adult, cooked in the oven and eaten.

SKILLS CHECKLIST

As you explore and study nature, you will also be learning helpful skills. While working through the book, use our checklist to keep track of your progress. Once you have checked off all of the activities for each category, you will be equipped with the important skills you need to be a true naturalist!

NOTICING

- Look Around You, page 4
- Map It Out, page 10
- Cabinet of Curiosities, page 16
- Out on a Limb, page 18
- Monet the Naturalist, page 20
- Signs of the Seasons, page 24
- For a Rainy Day, page 26
- Mostly Cloudy, page 28
- The Way of the Wind, page 34
- Sky Watch, page 36
- Around the Clock, page 38
- Moon Walk, page 42
- Magnifying Glass (of Water!), page 50

- The Great Backyard Bird Count, page 70
- Furry Friends, page 76
- Making Tracks, page 78
- Underwater View, page 82
- Wildlife Scavenger Hunt, page 84
- Snail Trail, page 86
- How to Read a Tree, page 90
- Breathing Tree, page 92
- A Dishful of Dandelions, page 102
- Fun with Fungus, page 104

ART AND CRAFTS

- Picture This, page 8
- Map It Out, page 10
- Take a Walk, page 12
- Cabinet of Curiosities, page 16

- Monet the Naturalist, page 20
- Mostly Cloudy, page 28
- Blow Wind Blow, page 32
- Seeing Stars, page 40

ADVENTURING

LANGUAGE ARTS

IDENTIFICATION

SURVIVAL

TINKERING

GLOSSARY

air pressure: the weight of air molecules pressing down on the earth

amphibians: cold-blooded animals with vertebra (backbones) and no scales

caecilian: a group of amphibians without arms or legs; they look similar to large worms

camouflage: to blend in or appear hidden with disguise

carnivore: an animal that eats meat

chlorophyll: the green coloring found in plants that absorbs energy from sunlight during the process of photosynthesis

chrysalis: the hard protective covering of a butterfly between the larva and adult stage

compost: a mixture of decayed organic matter often used for fertilizing gardens

coniferous: a tree with cone-like seeds that typically stays green year-round, such as pine, cypress, spruce, or cedar

decomposition: the process of rotting or decaying

dense: thick or packed tightly

displace: move from one place to another

Earth's crust: the outer layer of our planet

fauna: the animals found in a particular area

flora: the plants found in a particular area

forage: to pick or collect plants

gnomon: the part of a sundial that casts a shadow

habitat: the natural home of an animal, plant, or organism

herbivore: an animal that eats plants

hypothesis: an educated guess

inner core: the innermost layer of the Earth

insectivore: an animal that eats insects

larva: the in-between stage of an insect after it has left its egg, but is not yet an adult

mantle: a very hot, dense layer of the Earth; this is Earth's largest layer

metamorphosis: the process of changing from an immature form to an adult form through stages

naturalist: a scientist who studies nature

omnivore: an animal that eats both plants and animals

organic matter: matter from a recently living organism; in soil, this helps with plant growth

organism: a living thing, such as animals, plants, fungi, or bacteria

ornithologist: a scientist who studies birds

outer core: the second-to-last layer of the Earth, made of melted metals, such as nickel and iron

paleontologist: a scientist who studies fossils

permeable: allows gases and liquids to go through it

petrichor: the earthy smell produced when rain falls on dry ground

photosynthesis: the process of plants using energy from the sun to create their own food

pollination: dropping pollen onto a plant or flower to allow for fertilization

pollinator: an animal, such as a bee, butterfly, or bird, that visits a flower and carries its pollen to another flower

pollution: trash or other substances that are harmful to the environment

preserve: to keep something in its original state or condition

recycle: the process of turning waste into something usable

refraction: the change of direction, or bending of a ray (such as light), when it enters a different material

reproduce: to copy or make more of something

scatologist: a scientist who studies feces (poop)

sediment: the soft material made of tiny particles that fall to the bottom of a liquid

soil erosion: the wearing away of topsoil by wind or water

stomata: a tiny opening of a plant where gases and water vapor can pass through

whorl: the areas where branches grow from the trunk and circle around the tree

RESOURCES

Websites

Audubon: Guide to North American Birds. A wonderful resource for identifying birds and learning more information about a specific bird species. www.Audubon.org/Bird-Guide

The Cornell Lab of Ornithology: All About Birds. Here, you will be able to view live action from birdfeeder cameras, as birds from many different locations stop to eat. Cams.AllAboutBirds.org

Education.com: This site will help extend your study of earth science and other subjects. www.Education.com/Resources/Earth-Science

KidsGardening: Check out this website for additional gardening activities, growing guides, and educator resources. www.KidsGardening.org

National Geographic Kids: Here you will find science videos, games, nature facts, photos, and more—all created with kids in mind! www.Kids.NationalGeographic.com

Weather Wiz Kids: Meteorologist Crystal Wicker designed this kid-friendly website full of helpful information on weather and natural disasters. www.WeatherWizKids.com

Recommended Reading

Balanced and Barefoot by Angela J. Hanscom: Looks at the benefits of outdoor play in creating strong and confident children.

The Garden Classroom by Cathy James: Inspiration for taking literature, math, and science outdoors.

How to Raise a Wild Child by Scott D. Sampson: All about helping children fall in love with nature.

Last Child in the Woods by Richard Louv: Exploring the nature deficit of today's children and the effects we are seeing from it.

Make It Wild! by Fiona Danks and Jo Schofield: The authors offer 101 things to make and do outdoors.

INDEX

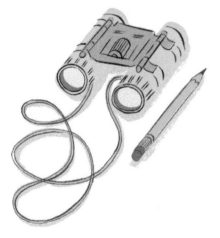

About the Author

 **KIM ANDREWS** is a North Carolina-based writer and blogger. She enjoys adventures by the river with her husband and their three children, is slightly obsessed with full moons, and thinks you can never have too many pet chickens. Kim studies environmental education, teaches nature classes on her family's small farm, and blogs about her passion for exploring, crafting, and outdoor learning at www.LearningBarefoot.com.